How to Prepare a
LEGAL
CITATION

About the Author

Elaine C. Maier received her J.D. degree from George Washington University in 1979 and is a member of the D.C. Bar. She has conducted seminars on cite-checking for the National Capital Area Paralegal Association and is presently an Associate with the Washington, D.C., law firm of Ingersoll and Bloch, Chartered. She is also on the faculty of the Georgetown University Legal Assistant Program and is a frequent lecturer with the Legal Education Institute of the Department of Justice.

How to Prepare a
LEGAL
CITATION

Elaine C. Maier, J.D.

BARRON'S EDUCATIONAL SERIES, INC.

All inquiries should be addressed to:

Barron's Educational Series, Inc.
250 Wireless Boulevard
Hauppauge, New York 11788

Library of Congress Catalog Card No. 83-11310

International Standard Book No. 0-8120-2960-7

Library of Congress Cataloging in Publication Data
Maier, Elaine C., 1946-
    How to prepare a legal citation.

    Includes index.
    1. Citation of legal authorities—United States—
Programmed instruction.   I. Barron's Educational
Series, Inc.   II. Title.   III. Title: How to prepare
a legal citation.
KF245.M34   1986   340'.072073   83-11310
ISBN 0-8120-2960-7
PRINTED IN THE UNITED STATES OF AMERICA

456   800   98765

Contents

Preface

My first lessons in cite-checking (and associated skills of using *Shepard's* and *A Uniform System of Citation*) were learned on the job by trial and error, generally under deadline pressure. In vain I searched for a manual to help guide me through the confusing maze of rules, exceptions, and variations that the Bluebook presented (in those days of the eleventh edition, examples were scanty). As I became more proficient in the skill, I was given more and more cite-checking assignments—so many that I could not handle the demand. I was then asked to give in-house training seminars for my paralegal colleagues, who lacked the experience I had obtained. A short time later, as production editor of a student-run law journal, I undertook the task of training first- and second-year law students to prepare articles for publication. I found that, except for on-the-job efforts such as mine, paralegals and law students had little formal training in this area and no textbooks to guide them. Yet law firms expected their law clerks, associates, secretaries, paralegals, and librarians to be experts in cite-checking.

In designing exercises for the seminars, I was struck with the idea of preparing a book—suitable for all those who found this area of their training neglected—that would describe each of the steps involved in putting a legal memorandum or brief into final form and that would provide exercises designed to develop familiarity and proficiency with the process.

This book is the result of that quest. It is the author's hope that this book will fill a gap in an area that is often omitted or given short shrift in legal education, will expand the role of the attorney's assistant, and will result in the preparation of better briefs, from the caption on the front cover to the final footnote.

Acknowledgments

The author gratefully acknowledges the following sources, for granting permission to reprint or adapt portions of the cited works:

1. The Harvard Law Review Association, *A Uniform System of Citation* (13th ed. 1981).
2. West Publishing Company, illustration in Chap. 2, *Federal Supplement* Advance Sheets for vols. 486 and 487 F. Supp. (printed matter on spines).
3. McGraw-Hill, Inc., illustrations in Chaps. 2 and 5, abbreviations and sample searches (reprinted from *Shepard's Atlantic Reporter Citations*, 1981 Annual Supplement, p. 528, and *Shepard's United States Citations—Statutes*, Supplement 1974–1979 to Statute Edition, 1968, p. 543).
4. Bureau of National Affairs, *United States Law Week*, vol. 48, pp. 3046, 3214, 3219, sample search in Chap. 2.

5. *Houston Law Review*, vol. 17, No. 4 (May 1980), "Texas' New Obscenity Laws: Redefining Taste," pp. 837, 847, 868, nn. 9, 61, 179; "Political, Social, and Economic Boycotts by Consumers: Do They Violate the Sherman Act?" pp. 795, 801, 802, 803, 806, 807, 825, 826, nn. 115, 159, 166, 183, 185, 281, 290, 291, 297; "The Conditions of Pretrial Confinement," p. 876, n. 18.

6. *Marquette Law Review*, vol. 64, No. 1 (Fall 1980), Stephen Mazurek, "Effects of Unemployment Compensation Proceedings on Related Labor Litigation," p. 141, n. 36.

7. *The Harvard Law Review*, vol. 95 (1982), "Developments in the Law: The Interpretation of State Constitutional Rights," pp. 1480, 1481, nn. 107, 113; Note, "Commercial Bank Mergers: The Case for Procedural and Substantive Deregulation," pp. 1914, 1916, 1917, nn. 11, 15; Note, "A Closer Look at Pendent and Ancillary Jurisdiction: Toward a Theory of Incidental Jurisdiction," p. 952, n. 100; Eisenberg, "The Bargain Principle and Its Limits," 95 Harv. L. Rev. 741, p. 778, n. 101.

8. *Loyola University of Chicago Law Journal*, vol. 12, No. 2 (1981), "OSHA's Rulemaking Authority under the OSHA: *Marshall v. American Petroleum Institute*," p. 238, n. 36; Note, "The Municipal Zoning Power and Section 1983 Liability after *Owen v. City of Independence*," pp. 211, 216, nn. 10, 31; Note, "Parallel State and Federal Court Class Actions," pp. 278, 279, nn. 5, 7; Jeffrey Fort, "The Necessary Demise of Federal Common Law Nuisance," pp. 141, 143, 155, nn. 54, 55, 67, 147; "*Harris v. McRae*, Indigent Women Must Bear the Consequences of the Hyde Amendment," p. 262, n. 51.

9. *Georgia Law Review*, vol. 15, No. 2 (Winter 1981), Note, "Business Necessity: Judicial Dualism and the Search for Adequate Standards," pp. 378, 393, nn. 10, 72; "Interpretation of 'Enterprise' under Rico: Legitimate Business Only?" p. 470, n. 9.

10. *The John Marshall Law Review*, vol. 14, No. 1 (Fall 1980), Casenotes, "*Katz v. Eli Lilly & Co.*, Limitation of Collateral Estoppel in Products Liability Litigation," p. 203, nn. 7, 11; "*Petrie v. Illinois High School Association:* Gender Classification and High School Athletics," p. 227.

11. *Oklahoma Law Review*, vol. 33, No. 2 (Spring 1980), Note, "Oil and Gas, Alienability of Lease-Granted Easements and Profits," pp. 430–32, nn. 1–15.
12. *Florida State University Law Review*, vol. 8, No. 1 (Spring 1980), Robert W. Martin, Jr., "Legislative Delegations of Power and Judicial Review—Preventing Judicial Impotence," p. 54, n. 49.

A SPECIAL ACKNOWLEDGMENT

In gratitude to the many people who have inspired me in this effort, especially the following:

To Mark Wine, Esq., of Kirkland and Ellis, who hired and trained me in my first paralegal position;

To Robert VanVoorhees, Esq., of Kirkland and Ellis, for encouraging me to pursue legal research and writing;

To James Wallace, III, Esq., Nolan Clark, Esq., Stephen Herman, Esq., Philip Davis, Esq., and numerous other attorneys at Kirkland and Ellis for supplying me with copious cite-checking assignments, and for demanding perfection;

To the National Capital Area Paralegal Association, for their continued support of this project and for supplying marketing suggestions;

To Sonja Marcum, for supplying publishing leads, general encouragement, and typing assistance;

To my fellow editors and staff members of the *George Washington Journal of International Law and Economics*, for providing rewarding publishing experiences;

To Patricia Brandel, for tirelessly typing and revising the manuscript;

To Susan Oglebay, Esq., for her proofreading and editorial suggestions;

To Robin Margolis, for her helpful comments on legislative materials;

To Stuart Marshall Bloch, Esq., of Ingersoll and Bloch, Chartered, for his invaluable advice and encouragement;

To Richard Charles Deering, Esq., for his continued love and moral support.

A special thanks to Michael B. Reuben, former executive editor of the *Harvard Law Review*, and final editor of *A Uniform System of Citation* (13th edition), for reviewing and criticizing the manuscript.

How to Use This Book

This book attempts to set forth, in an orderly fashion, each of the steps that must be carried out in an in-depth cite-checking assignment. It describes how to check legal citations for accuracy, locate missing or incomplete citations, update the citation through the use of *Shepard's* and *U.S. Law Week*, and put citations into the proper form, following the rules set forth in the Bluebook.

Each rule of citation is explained concisely and followed by one or more examples of its application. At the end of each subsection, an open-book exercise is given, consisting of several representative citations containing common errors in the area covered in the preceding subsection. This book is not intended to be used as a substitute for consulting the Bluebook but rather as an aid in becoming aware of and mastering its contents. Nor is the book designed to instruct the user to correct citations from memory but rather to encourage the use of the Bluebook whenever there is the slightest doubt. (Note that whereas the Bluebook illustrates the proper typeface to be used in typeset documents, this book shows the proper form when preparing typewritten documents.)

In addition, the book describes a myriad of other steps encountered in the cite-checking process: how to distinguish record citations from legal authorities, the proper form for direct quotations, the correct choice of introductory signals, how to set up a table of contents and table of authorities, how to structure footnotes in law review articles, and how to prepare material for printing. Although this book is not intended to be a manual on legal research, it will familiarize the user with the research tools necessary for the correction of inaccurate citations.

The book is suitable either for classroom use or as a self-teaching aid. It can be used as a basic manual for beginners, as an in-depth text for advanced students, or as a reference tool for the occasional cite-checker. In some chapters, the more obscure items are marked with a SINGLE ASTERISK (*), so that the learner may become aware of these items without spending an inordinate amount of time on them or may skip over these items and concentrate on the more commonly encountered citation problems.

RECOMMENDATIONS FOR USE

As a Self-teaching Aid. If this is your introduction to cite-checking, it is recommended that you read the Glossary and Chapters 1 through 6 and 8 in the order given, omitting the portions marked with single asterisks. You should complete each exercise at your own pace before going on to the next segment. The exercise using the sample memorandum that appears at the end of Chapter 8 (Exercise 2) is designed to review your cite-checking skills acquired from previous chapters and to familiarize you with the kind of cite-checking assignment you will encounter on the job. You may save the single-asterisked material and Chapters 7 and 9 for enrichment material to be used if additional time is available at the end of the course or later after you have gained further experience.

If you have had some experience in cite-checking, but would like to become more proficient at it, you will find the entire book useful as a review and manual on the finer points of cite-checking. Finally, if you are familiar with cite-checking but occasionally receive an assignment using unfamiliar sources, this book will be useful as a ready reference tool and quick teaching aid.

In the Classroom. In a classroom setting, this book may serve as a text for either an introductory or an advanced course in cite-checking and related skills, or may be used as a self-help supplement to a course in legal research and writing.

If, as a teacher, you are using the book as a text for beginners with little previous experience in cite-checking or legal research, it is suggested that students use the entire book, with the exception of the single-asterisked items appearing throughout the book, and omitting Chapters 7 and 9. For evaluation purposes, assign odd-numbered items within each exercise to be completed outside the classroom, as well as the following exercises, which must be performed at the library: Chapter 1, Exercises 2, 4; Chapter 2, Exercises 1, 2, 3, 4, 5; Chapter 3, Exercises 5, 6, 9; Chapter 5, Exercise 3; Chapter 6, Exercise 2; Chapter 7, Exercises 1, 2; Chapter 8, Exercise 2. (Exercise 3 in Chapter 2 can be performed in class if a copy of the *Jones v. United States* case is provided to each student.) The even-numbered items of the remaining exercises can be assigned as classroom open book quizzes. Exercise 2 in Chapter 8 may be assigned as a take-home test.

You may follow a similar plan for advanced students, assigning the single-asterisked material and Chapters 7 and 9 for study, saving the even-numbered items for review exercises to be assigned in the advanced level of the course, and assigning exercises following Chapters 7 and 9 as outside assignments.

This plan will reinforce skills previously acquired and should serve as a more effective mode of presentation than merely dividing the text into halves.

If you are using the text as a course supplement, you may wish to make outside assignments optional and compile a final test consisting of one or two items from each of the exercises that can be done outside of the library. For your convenience, an index to exercises that classifies the exercises for classroom or library use has been prepared. You will find it in the back part of this book.

It is the author's hope that instructors will find this book to be a flexible and effective teaching tool.

Important Notice on the Thirteenth Edition of the Bluebook

As this book was being written, the thirteenth edition of *A Uniform System of Citation* appeared, and several minor changes in citation form went into effect. For a summary of changes brought about by the new edition, see page v of the Bluebook.

Throughout this text, rules in citation that represent a departure from the twelfth edition are marked with a DOUBLE ASTERISK (**) to aid the experienced cite-checker in making the transition to the new edition. You should also be aware of the following changes in format:

1. The book is bound with a spiral binding, so that it will lie open more easily. It is *not* designed to accommodate replacement pages.
2. The inside front cover and facing page contain examples of basic citation forms for authorities cited in typewritten briefs

and in printed law review footnotes, illustrating the correct typeface to be used.

3. The inside back cover lists abbreviations to be used for geographical designations (U.S. and foreign) and for months of the year.

4. The lists of abbreviations for forming titles of periodicals have been consolidated into a single list.

5. The outer back cover contains a guide to the "tab index" by which the contents are organized.

6. The text contains more examples illustrating the rules of citation.

7. The index has been expanded to include more entries and contains references to both instructions and examples.

1 | *Introduction to Cite-Checking; The Use of Record Materials*

This chapter outlines each step involved in the cite-checking process, describes the parts of a brief, distinguishes record materials from legal authorities, illustrates the use of record materials, describes how to compile an appendix, and will familiarize the reader with special requirements imposed by local court rules.

A. SCOPE OF THE TASK

What does an attorney expect when he or she hands you a brief, legal memorandum, or law review article, in either rough or near-final form, and asks you to "check the cites"? The answer is that the expectation varies, depending on the submission deadline, how many revisions remain to be made, whether it's an intraoffice research memorandum or a printed brief to be filed in court, how compulsive the assigning attorney is, and how much attention the author paid to form. As the person responsible for the final form of the document, you may be expected to accomplish one or more of the following steps:

1. Proofread for accuracy and consistency.
2. Check the given citations against the sources cited.
3. If any citations are missing or incorrect, supply the correct cite (see Chapter 2.A.1).

4. Check all direct quotations word for word against the text (see Chapter 2.B).
5. Shepardize the cases to show further disposition on appeal (see Chapter 2.C).
6. Make sure that all citations conform to <u>A Uniform System of Citation</u> (see Chapters 3 to 6).
7. Read each case to make sure it supports the proposition for which it is cited (see Chapter 7).
8. Prepare an appendix of all record authorities cited in the memo (see Chapter 1.C).
9. Prepare a table of contents and table of authorities (see Chapter 8.B).
10. Make sure the format complies with any applicable court rules (see Chapter 1.D).
11. Proofread the memo through all subsequent drafts, changing footnote numbers and internal cross references if necessary (see Chapter 8.A).
12. If the brief is to be printed, prepare it for the printer and proofread the galleys against the manuscript (see Chapter 9).

Therefore, at the outset of the assignment, it is best to have a brief discussion with the responsible attorney about the scope of the task, the time limitations involved, and the degree of thoroughness required. If the memo is to go through numerous subsequent revisions, it might be best to postpone the cite-checking until it is closer to the final version. It is difficult to assess in advance how much time will be required to do the job properly, but a lengthy brief that has already been through several revisions (and has had more opportunities for typographical errors to be made) could take several days to put into final form, whereas a carefully written first draft may require only a few hours to verify the cites. You should also at this point gather the source materials used in preparation of the brief. It is likely that the principal author has his or her working materials still at hand and in some semblance of order.

B. PARTS OF THE BRIEF

The body of most legal briefs and memoranda of law contains three principal parts: a statement of facts, a summary of either law or legal arguments, and a conclusion. The statement of facts outlines (for the benefit of the judge) the factual situation in the case being discussed or argued. Depending on whether the memo is an impartial discussion of research on applicable case law or an advocacy piece submitted in the course of a lawsuit or administrative proceeding, the facts may be presented in a manner favorable to the party in whose behalf it is filed. In either event, the facts stated must be supported with references to the record developed in the course of the proceeding at hand. Such "record materials" may include allegations contained in the complaint, answer, counterclaim, or other pleadings; facts set forth in an affidavit or stipulation signed by one or more of the parties; statements given at a pretrial hearing or deposition; or information contained in a deposition exhibit, answers to interrogatories, or documents provided in response to a document request. If the memorandum or brief is being submitted on appeal of an agency or trial court decision, there may be references to the transcript or record of the proceeding below as well. This list, of course, is not exhaustive, and source material used to set forth the facts will vary, depending on the nature of the proceeding. The important distinction to keep in mind is that record materials are not legal authorities. They are given to show that there is a factual basis for the version of the facts presented for the case under consideration. They are unique to the case on which you are working and are a part of the court docket (or record). A final decision is pending.

Legal authorities, on the other hand, consist primarily of case law at the court or agency level in past cases (cited for their precedential value), statutes, rules and regulations, and secondary authorities such as treatises and law review articles. They can be found in the law library or obtained from the issuing court. When compiling a table of authorities, keep in mind that only legal authorities are included and not record materials in the case at hand. The purpose is to list all the materials cited as authority for the arguments being advanced.

C. THE USE OF RECORD MATERIALS

There is no prescribed form for the citation of record materials in a legal memorandum. Record materials are generally cited internally (in text), and an abbreviated form may be established for subsequent citations the first time a particular source is used.

EXAMPLE: Throughout the period of his probation, the defendant reported to his parole officer once a week, as required by the terms of his pretrial release. Pretrial Agency Report at p. 2 [hereinafter cited as "Report"].

In cite-checking this portion of a memorandum, simply check for consistency of format (every time you cite to the complaint, is it "Comp. ¶ 3" or "(Complaint, p. 6)"?), and verify from the original document that the quotation or statement is correct.

If the proceeding is lengthy or complex, or if the court rules require it, the attorney may wish to have an appendix assembled consisting of all record documents cited in the statement of facts. This will involve essentially three steps: gathering the record materials, identifying each document in the appendix by letter or numbering each page consecutively, and amending the statement of facts to include references to the appendix as well as the original document. For example, the complaint may now be identified as "Exhibit A" or "App. p. 13," and references to it would read "Comp. ¶ 3, Ex. A" or "Comp. ¶ 3, App. p. 13." All subsequent references to the complaint in the text of the memorandum must be consistent with the first reference.

If you are citing throughout the statement of facts to several pages of a voluminous transcript, you may find it convenient to assemble all quoted pages of the transcript in chronological order as a single exhibit. If the transcript covers more than one day, and each day the page numbering begins at page 1, you will need to indicate the date in the citation. Otherwise, for a three-day deposition, there may be three possible page 10's!

EXAMPLE: Smith Dep. Tr. at 88 (Aug. 7, 1975). Smith Dep. Tr. at 10 (Aug. 10, 1975).

The final step of the appendix process is to prepare an index to the record materials contained in it. In Illustration 1, the documents were assembled, and each page was consecutively numbered, beginning with page 1 on the first page of the complaint. To avoid confusion, each separate day of Smith testimony was listed as a separate entry. An alternative method would have been to refer to the complaint as "Exhibit A" (or "Appendix A"), to the summary judgment motion as "Exhibit B," and so forth.

ILLUSTRATION 1

Document	Appendix Page
Complaint (filed Jan. 30, 1975)	1
Plaintiff's Summary Judgment Motion (filed April 5, 1975)	5
Smith Deposition Testimony (August 5, 1975), pp. 33–35, 55, 88	10
Smith Deposition Testimony (August 6, 1975), pp. 22–27, 45–46, 62)	15

When a proceeding has reached the appellate stage, the judge may order the parties to compile a "joint appendix," consisting of all record materials from the trial level to be cited by each party in their briefs. Each party may be asked to submit a list of materials to a designated coordinator, who will then prepare a master list and assemble the documents. Each page will then be numbered in sequence, and citations will be to the joint appendix.

D. LOCAL COURT RULES

Another matter that should be looked into as early as possible is whether the court in which the memo is being filed has any applicable rules on format (for example, size of page, margins, color of cover for printed briefs; the preparation of any additional material such as a list of interested parties; or, in the table of authorities, marking with an asterisk those cases chiefly relied upon).

Part of a complete cite-checking job is to make sure all formal requirements of the court have been met. Keep in mind that some courts will reject a filing that is technically improper. Other courts will require the subsequent filing of a corrected pleading. At the very least, a poor impression is created on the judge and opposing parties if the party filing a pleading omits information required by the court. The importance of this step cannot be overlooked.

You should also ascertain in advance the deadline (date and time) for filing and serving the motion or brief, the number of copies required to be deposited with the clerk, and the form of certificate of service. If the filing is to be accomplished by mail, find out whether certified mail is required and the date by which the material must be postmarked. Finally, you will need to be aware of the procedure for obtaining a deadline extension, if necessary.

EXERCISE ☐1

Assume that the following record materials have been accurately cited as to content. Also assume that the memorandum containing the following statement of facts is to be submitted to the District of Columbia Superior Court, Criminal Division.

1. Correct the statement for consistency of citation form.
2. Compile an index to the appendix. Designate each day of the trial transcript cited in the statement as a separate entry and, following the illustration given in the text, determine the page number at which each exhibit begins. Exclude other entries.
3. Revise the citations to the transcript in text wherever necessary to refer to the appendix. (Use the form "App. at _____.")

STATEMENT OF FACTS

On October 10, 1977, Appellant was initially arrested by officers of the Metropolitan Police Department. (March 21 Tr. 140) Appellant was originally arrested at his home on a charge of assault. (March 21 Tr. 188) This charge arose out of an incident that took place on the evening of October 7, 1977, and early morning of October 8, 1977, March 21, Tr. 5, and involved Ms. Edna McConnell, the complainant, who had known Appellant for several years prior to the events of that night. (Tr. 6 March 21)

Beginning on October 11, 1977, Appellant was represented by John Drury, Esq. However, Mr. Drury's appearance was for the limited purpose of presentment only, (Dec. 6 Trans. 3), and the trial court appointed Grandison Hill, Esq., on October 21, 1977, to represent the Appellant. On November 29, 1977, Mr. Drury formally withdrew his appearance by praecipe and notified the trial court in person at the Appellant's arraignment on December 6, 1977, in CR 88377-77. (Dec. 6 Tr. 4)

While the case jacket indicates that Appellant was scheduled for arraignment in CR 88377-77 on November 29, 1977, the hearing held at that time was termed a "status hearing." (Nov. 29 Tr. 2) There was no plea entered in the matter until December 6, 1977. (Dec. 6 Tr. p. 5). By the time of the November 29, 1977 "status hearing," Appellant had already been in contact with Mr. Hill, his newly appointed counsel. In arguing for a mental examination, counsel noted that he had "several conversations" with Appellant. (Nov. 29 Tr. at 2) Despite this preliminary contact, or perhaps because of it, the Appellant became apprehensive about counsel's effectiveness in his case. As a consequence, Appellant filed a pro se motion alleging, inter alia, ineffectiveness of counsel (R. 23) (See Appendix A, Petition for Hearing)

At the arraignment hearing in CR 88377-77, held on December 6, 1977, appointed counsel was again not present to represent Appellant due to a friend's unspecified medical problems. (Dec. 6 Tr. 3) It should be noted that counsel also failed to appear for at least one hearing prior to the December 6th arraignment. (Nov. 29 Tr. 2) By a fortunate circumstance, Appellant's prior counsel, Mr. Drury, was present in court to explain the earlier appointment of Mr. Hill. (Dec. 6 Tr. 3) Thus, Mr. Drury stood in for appointed counsel at Appellant's arraignment on December 6, 1977. (Tr. 4 Dec. 6)

Although Appellant's trial was set for February 17, 1978 (Dec. 13 Tr. 4), because of the inability to complete the tests as required by the trial court, Appellant's trial was not begun until March 20, 1978. See letters at R. 136–138.

At trial, the government presented several witnesses. The major witness was Ms. Edna McConnell, the complainant, who recounted the events of October 7th and 8th of 1977. (Mar. 20 Tr. at 5) She testified concerning the threats which she said Appellant had made to her that evening. (Mar. 20 Tr. 18) The government presented testimony from several acquaintances of Appellant, as well as the police officers who initially arrested Appellant. The Government also presented physical evidence and photographs to support its case.

The Appellant testified in his own behalf and presented two additional witnesses. During the Appellant's testimony, he denied he threatened the complainant (Mar. 21 Tr. 233), and stated that at the time of the event he was in an alcoholic stupor. (Mar. 21, Tr. at p. 249) The defense also presented the testimony of Appellant's wife, (Mar. 22 p. 337) and Doctor Leonard Maitland of the District's Forensic Psychiatry Division. (Mar. 22 Tr. 313)

Dr. Maitland submitted a report which found Appellant competent to stand trial and indicated that his actions were not the product of mental illness. [See Appendix B, Defendant's Exhibit 2, also at R. 151]

This report was received, without government objection, by the trial court as part of Appellant's case in chief. (Mar. 22—Tr. 316) Dr. Maitland also indicated in his report that Appellant's behavioral controls "were probably impaired at the time of the offense" by alcohol. [Appendix 2, paragraph 5]

After two and one half days of deliberation, the jury found Appellant not guilty of obstructing justice (Mar. 28 Tr. 391) and reported a deadlock on the assault charge. (Mar. 28 Tr. 390) The jury did find the Appellant guilty of the charge of threats. (Mar. 28 Tr. 391) Appellant's counsel then requested a jury poll on the guilty verdict of threats. The first juror questioned on the "threats" verdict announced "not guilty." (Mar. 28 Tr. 391) The trial court proposed to continue the poll over the Appellant's objection. (Mar. 28 Tr. 391) After it was explained what a jury poll is designed to do, the first juror then announced "guilty." (Mar. 28, Tr. 392) The court concluded that the verdict was unanimous. (Mar. 28 Tr. 394) It also declared a mistrial as to the deadlocked assault charge. (Mar. 28 Tr. 394)

Appellant was scheduled to be sentenced on May 12, 1978, (Mar. 28 Tr. 395). On May 9, 1978, Mr. Hill was allowed to withdraw as counsel by the trial court, "at the defendant's request." (R. 7, 8) New counsel was appointed and Appellant was sentenced on May 11, 1978, to 4–12 years on the charge of threats. Appellant filed a pro se notice of appeal on May 18, 1978.

EXERCISE 2

Refer to the statement of facts in Exercise 1, and answer the following questions concerning additional requirements imposed by local court rules.

1. In filing a statement of points and authorities with the Superior Court of the District of Columbia, citations to cases decided by the

_____ [name of court] shall indicate the volume and page number of both U.S. App. D.C. reports and the Federal Reporter. [Rule 47-I(b)]

EXAMPLE: North Central Truck Lines, Inc. v. ICC, 182 U.S. App. D.C. 181, 559 F.2d 802 (1977).

NOTE: All cases decided by the United States Circuit Court for the District of Columbia Circuit are printed separately in a volume referred to as "U.S. App. D.C." (a West publication), as well as included in the Federal Reporter.)

2. Most motions in criminal proceedings must be filed within ten days of arraignment or entry of appearance of counsel, whichever is later, except for the following: (1) motions to dismiss for lack of speedy trial, (2) motions for release on conditions, (3) motions for review of conditions of release, (4) motions for reduction of bond or collateral, and (5) motions for _____. [Rule 47-I(c)]

3. Any motion for hearing must include a request that the hearing be set at least ____ days before the trial date. [Rule 47-I(d)]

4. Service of motions is normally made upon the _____ representing a party and filed with the court. [Rules 49(b) and (d)]

5. Papers in criminal actions shall be filed in the same manner provided for in _____ actions. [Rule 49(d)] These rules are found at Rule 10 of the Civil Rules of the Superior Court—Form of Pleadings.

6. Papers filed with the D.C. Superior Court shall be submitted on ____ -inch paper. [Rule 10-I(a)—Civil]

7. The first pleading filed in a case by either party shall include in the caption the name and home address of that party. If the party is not represented by counsel, _____ shall also be included. [Rule 10-I(b)—Civil]

8. If a party is represented by counsel, subsequent pleadings need not indicate the *party's* address and phone number but must include the *attorney's* name, office address and phone number, and _____ _____. [Rule 10-I(b)—Civil]

EXERCISE ③

Assume that the following record materials are accurately cited as to content. Also assume that the brief containing this statement of facts is to be submitted to the U.S. Court of Appeals for the District of Columbia Circuit.

1. Correct the statement for consistency of citation form.

2. Prepare an index to the appendix, listing all pages in the record cited in the statement, all pages in the opinion cited in the statement, and any other exhibits.

STATEMENT OF FACTS

Appellants in this action are Amy Young and Thomas Young t/a The American Food Store, hereinafter referred to as the "Thomases" or "American Food Store" or Defendants. Appellees in this action are

1800 Connecticut Avenue Joint Venture, hereinafter "1800 Connecticut Avenue Joint Venture" or "Plaintiff" where appropriate. The Record will be referred to as "R" followed by the corresponding page number in the transcript. The Court's Opinion will be referred to as "O" followed by the corresponding page number.

In July 1978, 1800 Connecticut Avenue Joint Venture purchased two adjacent parcels of real property in the District of Columbia, 1800 Connecticut Avenue and 2031 Florida Avenue, from Dr. Melvin McCarthy, his wife and his mother, May McCarthy. [R-15, 60, 61, 73]

Prior to July 1978, 1800 Connecticut Avenue was owned by Dr. Melvin McCarthy and his wife. (R-60, 61). Prior to July, 1978, the real property located at 2031 Florida Avenue was subject to a life interest in Mrs. May McCarthy with the remainder interest in her son, Dr. Melvin McCarthy. [R-73]

The Thomases began renting the property at 1800 Connecticut Avenue from Dr. Melvin McCarthy beginning May 1, 1974, at a rent of $225 a month. [Rec. 16, 18, 45, 75, Plaintiff's Exhibit 1]. The lease contained an option to renew for another three-year term at a monthly rental which was to be determined at the expiration of the lease. [Plaintiff's Exhibit 1] In June, 1977, the rent was increased to $250/month. [R 261] The lease of the American Food Store was for three years and expired on April 30, 1977. [R-1, 16, 18; Plaintiff's Exhibit 1]

After April 30, 1977, the Thomases became month-to-month tenants. [R-17, O-3] The Thomases did not exercise their option to renew their lease for another three-year term. [R-16, 47, 74, 267]

The property adjacent to the American Food Store, 2031 Florida Avenue, was rented by William Nathan and Perry White from May 4, 1974, to April 30, 1975, and operated under the name of American Bazaar. [R-1, 159, Plaintiff's Exhibit 6]. When Nathan and White left, the Thomases continued paying rent. [R-206]

On November 30, 1978, 1800 Connecticut Avenue Joint Venture gave the Thomases a 30-day notice to vacate. [R-18, 19, Plaintiff's Exhibit 2]. At the time of the trial, May 16, 1979, the Thomases were still in possession of the subject property. [O-3]

On April 8, 1978, the Thomases went to the residence of Mrs. McCarthy and asked her for a lease covering the premises at both 1800 Connecticut Avenue and 2031 Florida Avenue. [R-68, 177, 178] It was undisputed that Defendants owed back rent on both of the properties. [R-76, 77, 209, R-210]

One hundred ten dollars was due her son, Dr. Melvin McCarthy, for the eleven months that the American Food Store was paying $240/

month rent instead of $250/month for the property located at 1800 Connecticut. [R-70, 74] Eighteen hundred ten dollars was due on the property at 2031 Florida Avenue for back rent to which Mrs. May McCarthy was entitled. [R-140, 209, 266]

According to the Thomases' testimony and that of William Nathan, Mrs. McCarthy promised them a lease if they would pay the back rent. [R-153, 196, 270] The Thomases gave Mrs. May McCarthy a check for $110 for the back rent on 1800 Connecticut Avenue, which was deposited to the account by her son. [R-229] The Thomases sent Mrs. McCarthy a check for $1,810 for back rent on 2031 Florida Avenue for the American Bazaar. R-250.

Mrs. May McCarthy never gave them the lease. [R-152, 153] Furthermore, no rent of $500 a month was ever paid for the leasing of the two properties subsequent to the April 1978 meeting. (R-154, 227)

On November 30, 1978, 1800 Connecticut Avenue Joint Venture Associates gave the Thomases the 30-day notice to vacate. [R-18, 19] This appeal followed.

EXERCISE [4]

Refer to the statement of facts in Exercise 3, and answer the following questions concerning additional requirements imposed by the D.C. Circuit Court of Appeals. Be sure to consult the applicable court rule concerning the appendix to the briefs.

1. In the D.C. Circuit, the form of printed briefs, appendixes, petitions, and motions is governed by the

_____.

[Rule 8(a)]
2. In the table of authorities in briefs filed in the D.C. Circuit, cases or authorities chiefly relied on are

_____.

[Rule 8(b)]
3. The certificate required by Rule 8(c) shall include a list of

_____.

4. If an appendix of applicable statutes and regulations is filed pursuant to Rule 8(d), it may be bound within the covers of the brief in the form of

_____.

5. Rule 8(e) only applies to briefs filed by _____.

6. Rule 8(f) requires a parallel citation to _____ [name of reporter] when citing a decision of the court of the D.C. Circuit.

7. Principal briefs filed in the D.C. Circuit (except by permission of the court) may not exceed ____ pages. [Rule 8(h)]

8. An appellant must file ____ copies of the appendix with the D.C. Court of Appeals. [Rule 9(a)]

2 | *Using Legal Citations— Introduction*

This chapter describes the process of checking citations from the original source, tells how to locate the correct citation if the given citation is inaccurate or incomplete, lists the correct source to be cited, demonstrates the correct form for direct quotations, explains the Shepardizing process, illustrates the use of U.S. Law Week, sets forth the rules for including prior and subsequent history of a case, and explains the use of short forms for citing cases and statutes.

After you have completed proofreading the document once for typographical errors and have checked all record citations, you are ready to begin the legwork of checking the legal citations. This consists of locating the original source of the citation and checking it against the citation in the memorandum for accuracy and obtaining whatever additional information is necessary to complete the citation.

You can save yourself a great deal of time by obtaining, at the outset, copies of any source materials made by the principal authors (such as photocopies of cases or legislative histories) or utilizing the volumes consulted before they are returned to the library. A thoughtful attorney will save all materials used and transfer these to the cite-checker's office or to a conference room.

The following discussion is based on federal court cases, but the same principles can be applied to state court cases, using state and regional materials.

A. CHECKING THE CITES FOR ACCURACY AND COMPLETENESS

1. Finding the Correct Citation

Once you have completed the statement of facts of your memo or brief, you are ready to go to the library to look up the legal authorities cited. At a minimum, your task will be to verify each given citation by checking the actual source material cited.

The first step is to locate the cited volume on the shelf. With a copy of the case in front of you, turn to the first page of the case to verify the name of the case, the volume, page number, name of the reporter, the court, and the year the case was decided.

If a memorandum has already been through several typed drafts, or if it was hastily compiled from secondary sources (such as opponents' briefs or case blurbs in legal digests), you may find many incorrect case citations. Part of your job will be to locate the correct cite. As you will be pleased to learn, there are many time-saving methods of accomplishing this.

(a) Time-saver No. 1. Check the index to cases in the front of the book. If the volume number is correct but the page number is incorrect, you will find the correct citation immediately.

(b) Time-saver No. 2. You may be able to tell by looking at the citation that you are being led to the wrong reporter. U.S. district court cases (trial level) appear in the Federal Supplement (F. Supp.). U.S. circuit court cases (appellate level) appear in the Federal Reporter (F.2d). If the citation is to a district court case but refers to F.2d, try looking in the same volume of F. Supp. You may find the correct case instantly.

(c) Time-saver No. 3. Check the alphabetical table of cases at the end of the current Modern Federal Practice Digest or relevant state or regional digest. Unless it's a very recent case, you should find it right away. As always, check the pocket part supplement (a separately printed update to the main volume) which is inserted in the inside back cover. Failure to do so may result in an inaccurate or incomplete citation, since material in the pocket part may render the main volume obsolete.

> NOTE: If one of the parties is the United States or an agency, you may come across several cases of the same name. Take heart—you needn't check every case to find the correct cite. Simply look at the court issuing the opinion until you identify the case you want.

(d) Time-saver No. 4 (for recent cases). Consult the pocket part of the table-of-cases volume of the Modern Federal Practice Digest (or the applicable regional digest). If you cannot locate your case there, go to the advance sheets of the Digest (separately bound paperback volumes containing information on current cases). These volumes update entries for the entire Digest. A table of cases will appear at the back of each volume. As each advance sheet picks up where the last one left off, check each advance sheet on the shelf.

(e) Time-saver No. 5 (for very recent cases). Go to the case index in front of the pastel-colored advance sheets of the reporter in which the case is to be published. (See Illustration 2.) There may be several advance sheets on the shelf, but you will have to check only every third or fourth one, because the *index* for each volume is cumulative.

> HINT: If you look at the spine of each advance sheet, you will find the volume number of the reporter when hardbound, followed by the page numbers included in the advance sheet. These page numbers will not change in the hardbound edition, but several advance sheets will be replaced by a single hardbound volume. At the bottom of the spine will appear consecutive numbers in boldface type. Make sure all advance sheets are arranged in order on the shelves; then check only the most recent advance sheet for each hardbound volume.

In the examples shown in Illustration 2, you will need to check only No. 26 (index to volume 486) and No. 29 (index to volume 487). The index will indicate the page on which the case begins, which you can locate by looking at the spine of the remaining advance sheets in the series.

There is a remote danger in citing to cases published in advance sheets that the publisher may, at the last minute, substitute a recent (but different) opinion of the same length in the hardbound version. Thus, when time permits, all case citations obtained from advance sheets should be verified according to the permanently bound edition. If the cited case fails to appear in the hardbound edition, you should cite to the slip opinion.

(f) Time-saver No. 6. When all else fails, try looking in the table of cases, reversing the names of the parties. If you are unable to find the case at all, there may be an error in the case name, the name of the case may have changed on appeal, or the decision may not be printed in the West reporter system. (Not every decision is.) If no published version of a case is available, cite to the slip opinion issued by the court or agency, as shown in Section A.2(*h*) following.

ILLUSTRATION 2

486 F. Supp. No. 3	487 F. Supp. No. 2	487 F. Supp. No. 3	487 F. Supp. No. 4
Pages 934 to 1380	Pages 109 to 709	Pages 710 to 1368	Pages 1369 to 1391
487 F. Supp. No. 1			488 F. Supp. No. 1
Pages 1 to 108			Pages 1 to 544
26	**27**	**28**	**29**

NOTE: Reprinted from *Federal Supplement* Advance Sheets for Volumes 486 and 487 (printed matter on spines), with permission of the copyright holder. Copyright 1980 by West Publishing Company.

EXERCISE 1

The following citations are all incorrect; thus you may skip the step of locating the cited volume on the shelf. Using the hints given in the preceding chapter, locate the correct cite. Complete the citation if necessary.

1. Robinson-Patterson Coal Co. v. Morgan, 288 P. 335 (Kan. 1930).
2. Crossroads State Bank v. Savage, 436 F.2d 743 (W.D. Okla. 1977).
3. In re Penn Central Transportation Co., 449 F.2d 270.
4. Tidewater Oil Co. v. Penix, 232 F. Supp. 215.
5. McGee v. Estelle, ____ F.2d ____ (5th Cir. 1980).

2. Finding the Official Cite

Case decisions may be printed in any of several reporters. In order to cite to the correct source or sources, you will need to understand the difference between "official," "unofficial," and "preferred unofficial" reporter.

(a) Official Reports. Official reports are printed by the court issuing the opinion, out of funds provided by the legislature. For example, the official cite for Supreme Court cases is U.S. Reports. (These are published by the Supreme Court.)

Each federal government agency or commission publishes its own decisions in a reporter, which is frequently named after the agency (examples: FTC, ICC). These are also official citations.

Beginning at page 136 of the Bluebook, there appears a state-by-state rundown of both official and unofficial volumes containing decisions of the courts of that state and their dates of publication. The highest level court is listed first. Each state has two or three levels of courts, any of which may publish its decisions separately. Many of the highest and intermediate-level opinions are reprinted in West's regional reporters as well. In some states (for example, Texas), official reports are no longer published.

(b) Unofficial Reports. All commercially published reporters (such as West's, Lawyers' Co-operative Publishing Company, and BNA) contain unofficial reports. The "preferred unofficial" source to be cited is West's. In states in which official reporters are no longer published (for example, Tennessee), the state court may declare that West's regional reporter is henceforth the official reporter. In those states, West's is the only published source available.

Now that you are aware of the sources of official and unofficial cites, be aware that the Bluebook lists a number of rules on which source or sources to cite. As you have seen, particular court rules may impose additional citation requirements. Following is a summary of the Bluebook rules, followed by hints on how to find the official cite.

(c) United States Supreme Court. Cite only to the official reporter (U.S.) if available. Do not give a parallel citation.

RIGHT: United States v. Seatrain Lines, 329 U.S. 424 (1947).

WRONG: United States v. Seatrain Lines, 329 U.S. 424, 91 L. Ed. 396, 67 S. Ct. 435 (1947).

Of all the versions available, the official reporter is the latest to appear. If U.S. Reports are not yet available, cite to West's Supreme Court Reporter.

EXAMPLE: United States v. Seatrain Lines, 67 S. Ct. 435 (1947).

If you are citing to a very recent case, cite to U.S. Law Week, Supreme Court edition, published by BNA. Supreme Court opinions are published within a week or two of issuance.

EXAMPLE: Costle v. Pacific Legal Foundation, 48 U.S.L.W. 4243 (U.S. Mar. 18, 1980).

> HINTS: If you do not have the official cite, but know the date of the decision, you can locate the official version by looking at the cover of the advance sheets of U.S. Reports or the spine of the hardbound edition to determine in which volume the case is located. Then check the index to cases within.
>
> For older decisions, if you look at the beginning of the opinion in Lawyer's Edition or the West version, the parallel citation to the official reporter will be given. You can also check the table of cases in Modern Federal Practice Digest.

(d) Federal District or Appellate Courts. Cite to the following West reporters:

1. Federal Reporter [F., F.2d]—for U.S. circuit court opinions, Court of Claims, Court of Customs and Patent Appeals, Emergency Court of Appeals.
2. Federal Supplement [F. Supp.]—for U.S. district court opinions.
3. Federal Cases [F. Cas.]—for opinions of either the federal district or circuit courts prior to 1932.
4. Federal Rules Decisions [F.R.D.]—for opinions construing federal rules of procedure. If the opinion also appears in F. Supp., cite only to F. Supp. instead.

> HINTS: All opinions appearing in the West federal reporters are indexed in the table of cases of the Modern Federal Practice Digest, from the district court level through the Supreme Court level.
>
> Parallel citations to Supreme Court cases can be found by consulting Shepard's United States Citations. (Detailed instructions on the use of Shepard's appear in Part C of this chapter.)
>
> If an opinion appears in a loose-leaf service or other non-West publication, the index to that publication will usually indicate whether the case also appears in the West edition.

(e) State Court Opinions. As described previously, when citing to a state court decision, check the table in the Bluebook to ascertain the availability of both official and unofficial cites. Cite first to the official source, if available, and then give the parallel citation to West's regional reporter.

EXAMPLE: <u>Marmah, Inc. v. Town of Greenwich</u>, 176 Conn. 116, 405 A.2d 63 (1978).

Certain New York and California cases are separately printed in two additional West reports (<u>New York Supplement</u> and <u>California Reporter</u>). For those cases, give a *triple cite*, citing to the special reporter last.

EXAMPLE: Union Insurance Agency v. Holz, 2 N.Y.2d 727, 138 N.E.2d 729, 57 N.Y.S.2d 364 (1956).

EXAMPLE: <u>Pressman v. Temin</u>, 60 Cal. 2d 208, 359 P.2d 35, 50 Cal. Rptr. 47 (1960).

> HINT: The quickest way to find a parallel citation to a state court case is to look at the case caption given at the beginning of the opinion in the West version. Or you can check the alphabetical table of cases appearing at the end of the regional digests published by West. Other ways to get a parallel citation are by using <u>Shepard's</u> or by consulting the table of cases at the beginning of the volume in which the case appears. Finally, the <u>National Reporter Blue Book</u> will lead you from the official to the unofficial cite.

(f) Administrative Proceedings. Many government agencies have been created by statute and conferred with the authority to initiate proceedings against those in violation of statutes the agency is empowered to enforce. For example, the Securities and Exchange Commission (SEC) may initiate an enforcement action against a party violating the federal securities laws. The case is initially heard before an administrative law judge (formerly called a hearing officer), and the initial decision may be appealed to the agency commissioners. Depending on the enabling statute, the final agency opinion may be challenged in either the federal district or appellate courts.

Agency opinions are published initially as slip opinions, official releases, or unbound reports that indicate the volume number of the bound version. These opinions will eventually appear in official administrative reporters. A list of these reporters appears beginning at page 135 of the Bluebook. Many of these decisions are also reprinted in loose-leaf services.

(1) When citing to agency opinions, cite to the official reporter or to an official release. Note that often only the name of the respondent is given.

EXAMPLE: Tennessee Intrastate Rates & Charges, 286 I.C.C. 41 (1952).

EXAMPLE: Central & Southwest Corp., SEC Holding Co. Act Release No. 13,130 (March 14, 1956).

(2) When citing to an unbound report in which the pages have not yet been numbered, indicate the case number and give the date in full.

EXAMPLE: Guy Paschal, 29 T.C. No. 12 (Oct. 22, 1966).

(3) If the official reporter is not yet available in bound form, provide a parallel citation to an unofficial reporter or loose-leaf service.

EXAMPLE: Northern Natural Gas Co., FPC Op. No. 491, [Federal— New Matters] Util. L. Rep. (CCH) ¶ 10,718 (May 25, 1966).

Once the bound version of the official reporter is available, the citation would read as follows:

EXAMPLE· Northern Natural Gas Co., 35 F.P.C. 790 (1966).

HINT: The table of cases in the loose-leaf services contains information on the official citation.

For further information on how to cite agency proceedings, see Chapter 3.E.3.

(g) Order of Preference. If a case does not appear in either an official or a preferred unofficial version, cite to the following, in descending order of preference:

1. Another unofficial reporter (for example: Supreme Court Cases, Lawyer's Edition).
2. A loose-leaf service.
3. A periodical.
4. A newspaper.

The particular format for citations to these sources will be detailed in subsequent chapters.

(h) Unreported Cases. Unreported cases (cases appearing only in slip opinions issued by the court itself) have a special citation form that includes the docket number and full date of the opinion.

EXAMPLE: <u>Dodd v. Smith</u>, No. 74–329 (D. Mass. Jan. 21, 1975).

To cite to a particular page of the slip opinion, use the following form:

EXAMPLE: <u>Dodd. v. Smith</u>, No. 74–329, slip op. at 6 (D. Mass. Jan. 21, 1975).

***(i) Specially Reproduced Materials.* Some materials may be available only in such forms as microfilm, microfiche, computer print-outs, or a printed copy of material obtained on a computer terminal. You should parenthetically include in your citation to such material any information that would aid in its location or retrieval.

EXAMPLE: <u>Pennsylvania v. Environmental Protection Agency</u>, No. 79–1025 (3d Cir. Sept. 22, 1981) (available Mar. 1, 1982, on LEXIS, Genfed library, App. file).

(j) Pending Cases. Cases that have not yet been decided or that have not yet been finally adjudicated are cited similarly to unreported cases. You would indicate in the parentheses or elsewhere in the citation the significance of the date given.

EXAMPLE: <u>Dodd v. Smith</u>, No. 74–329 (D. Mass. filed Sept. 9, 1974).
EXAMPLE: <u>Dodd v. Smith</u>, No. 74–329 (D. Mass. Oct. 10, 1974) (order granting preliminary injunction).

In the first example, the date given was the date the complaint was filed.

In all cases in which a decision has been made at the trial court level, but an appeal is pending, the full date of the latest disposition in the appeal is included, and the docket number of the appellate forum is given in parentheses at the end of the citation.

EXAMPLE: Frissell v. Rizzo, 597 F.2d 840 (3d Cir. 1978), petition for cert. filed, 48 U.S.L.W. 3046 (U.S. Aug. 7, 1979) (No. 78–1890).

In this example, the docket number given is the number assigned by the U.S. Supreme Court.

EXERCISE ☐2

In the following examples, replace the unofficial citation with the correct official citation, or add the official citation to the given citation, whichever is appropriate. (Do not leave blanks.) Verify your findings by locating the correct volume on the shelf.

1. United Jewish Organizations of Williamsburgh, Inc. v. Carey, 45 U.S.L.W. 4221 (U.S. Mar. 1, 1977).
2. Branzburg v. Hayes, 33 L. Ed. 2d 626 (1972).
3. Carlson v. Green, 100 S. Ct. 1468 (1980).
4. City of Brookfield v. Wisconsin Employment Relations Commission, ____ Wis. 2d ____, 275 N.W.2d 723 (1979).
5. Hur v. City of Poughkeepsie, ____ App. Div. 2d 420 N.Y.S.2d ____, 414 (1979).
6. Civil Service Association v. City of San Francisco, ____ Cal. 3d ____, ____ P.2d ____, 150 Cal. Rptr. 129 (1978).
7. United States v. Azzarelli Construction Co., [1980–1] Trade Cas. (CCH) ¶ 63,103 (E.D. Ill. 1979).
8. Gowdy v. Richter, [1971–1978 Transfer Binder] Blue Sky L. Rep. (CCH) ¶ 71,152 (E.D. Ill. 1974).
9. Colonial Alloys Co. v. Kinkead Industries, 186 U.S.P.Q. 403 (N.D. Ill. 1975), aff'd, 539 F.2d 712 (7th Cir. 1976).
10. Smiertka v. IRS, 44 Ad. L. 2d (P & F) 737 (D.D.C. 1978).

B. USE OF DIRECT QUOTATIONS

All direct quotations must be checked word for word against the text of the opinion, and a citation to the page on which the quotation appears (called a "pinpoint cite" or "jump cite") *must* be given. The pinpoint cite immediately follows the page on which the case begins.

EXAMPLE: As the court stated in <u>United States v. Morris</u>, 491 F. Supp. 222, 225 (S.D. Ga. 1980), "[d]irect observation is not essential to the existence of probable cause."

When a point is made repeatedly throughout an entire source, either cite to the work as a whole (omitting the pinpoint cite), or use <u>passim</u> after the first page, as follows:

EXAMPLE: 405 U.S. 330 <u>passim</u> (1972).

If the pinpoint cite is not given in the memo, or the cite given is incorrect, skim through the headnotes or syllabus appearing at the beginning of the opinion to find the statement most closely approximating the quote.

*You should be aware of the distinction between headnotes and the court syllabus. Headnotes, consisting of consecutively numbered summaries of points of law contained in the case that follows, are prepared by the publisher and, although useful as a means of locating cases on a certain point, are not dispositive of the law. The syllabus of the court, on the other hand, is prepared by the clerk of the court and, in addition to being useful in locating points made in the case that follows, often has the force of law. A headnote may never be cited as authority for a statement made; a syllabus may be. However, it is preferable to cite from the text of the opinion itself.

In the West reporter system, each headnote will be numbered consecutively beginning with number 1, followed by a boldface topic and key number. For purposes of tracking down quotations, ignore the key number and refer only to the headnote number. When you have located the applicable headnote, search through the text of the opinion and look for a corresponding bracketed number at the beginning of selected paragraphs. That will identify the portion of the opinion from which the headnote was extracted. *Headnotes are not direct quotes, and should not be used to check a direct quote but only as an aid in locating the source of the quote.*

Following is a step-by-step guide to learning the correct style for direct quotations and for indicating any variation from the original text.

1. Basic Quotation Styles

(a) Short Quotations. Enclose short quotations (forty-nine words or fewer) in quotation marks and do not set off the quoted matter from the rest of the text. In nonblock quotes, commas and periods are always placed inside quotation marks. All other marks appear inside the quotation marks only if they are part of the quoted material. The citation will immediately follow the quote.

EXAMPLE: As the court noted in <u>Mighty Payloader</u>, forfeiture statutes have "an extraordinarily broad scope." <u>United States v. Twenty-Eight "Mighty Payloader" Gaming Devices</u>, 623 F.2d 510, 516 (8th Cir. 1980).

(b) Lengthy Quotations (block quotes). Indent quotations of fifty words or more five spaces in from both right and left margins, and do *not* enclose within quotation marks. The block quote should also be single-spaced. The fact that it is indented and single-spaced will signify that the set-off material is a direct quote. Repeat the punctuation in the original (including single or double quotation marks) faithfully.

EXAMPLE:

> The Government argues that the district court erred in not requiring the seized items to be forfeited under 26 U.S.C. §§ 7301, 7302. The district court held there are unique circumstances in this case which would make it fundamentally unfair for the Government to take the machines from their owners without first giving them the opportunity to pay the tax.

(c) Citations Following Block Quotes. After you have quoted the last word from the original source, skip a space and indicate the source of the quotation, going back to the margin of the text. That way, it will be clear that the citation is the source of the quote and is not a part of the quote itself:

EXAMPLE:

> The Government contends that section 7302 does not allow a good faith defense. Having determined the machines are subject to the tax imposed by 26 U.S.C. § 4461 and the tax was not paid, it is clear the property has been used in violation of the internal revenue laws and is subject to forfeiture.

Forfeiture statutes have an extraordinarily broad scope. United States v. United States Coin & Currency, 401 U.S. 715, 91 S.Ct. 1041, 28 L.Ed.2d 434 (1971).
United States v. Twenty-Eight "Mighty Payloader" Gaming Devices, 623 F.2d 510, 516 (8th Cir. 1980).

NOTE: In this example, the Mighty Payloader case (the cite given immediately after the block quote) is the source of the quotation, and United States v. United States Coin & Currency is a case citation appearing within the Mighty Payloader case.

2. Use of Indentation to Show Paragraph Structure of the Original Source

(a) Further Indentation of Quoted Matter. If the quoted material begins a paragraph in the original text, further indent the first sentence of the paragraph in the block quote.

EXAMPLE:

The district court determined the machines are coin-operated gaming devices. The district court's findings, that successful operation of these machines involves a substantial element of chance, that prizes greater than the value of the cost of a play can be obtained, and that the machines are coin-operated, are not clearly erroneous.

(b) Words Left Out at the Beginning of a Paragraph. If the original quotation is taken from the middle of a paragraph, do not indent the first word of the quote. The entire quotation will be aligned in block style.

EXAMPLE:

The district court held there are unique circumstances in this case which would make it fundamentally unfair for the Government to take the machines from their owners without first giving them the opportunity to pay the tax. The court discussed the following equitable considerations: (1) the IRS' failure to attempt to collect taxes on these types of machines generally; and (2) persons in the carnival business were unaware or misled by conduct and statements made by agents of the IRS.

(c) Entire Paragraph Deleted. When skipping over and *deleting entirely* one or more paragraphs, insert and indent four periods (separated by spaces), and begin the next paragraph on the next line.

EXAMPLE:

The district court determined the machines are coin-operated gaming devices. The district court's findings, that successful operation of these machines involves a substantial element of chance, that prizes greater than the value of the cost of a play can be obtained, and that the machines are coin-operated, are not clearly erroneous.

. . . .

26 U.S.C. § 7302 provides:

It shall be unlawful to have or possess any property intended for use in violating the provisions of the internal revenue laws, or regulations prescribed under such laws, or which has been so used, and no property rights shall exist in any such property.

(d) Words Left Out at the Beginning of a Subsequent Paragraph. When quoting more than one paragraph, and when deleting language at the beginning of a *second or subsequent* paragraph in a quote, insert and indent three periods (separated by spaces) to indicate ellipsis (words left out). Do not follow this rule if words are left out at the beginning of the *first* paragraph in a quote. Instead, see Step 2(*b*).

EXAMPLE:

The district court determined the machines are coin-operated gaming devices. The district court's findings, that successful operation of these machines involves a substantial element of chance, that prizes greater than the value of the cost of a play can be obtained, and that the machines are coin-operated, are not clearly erroneous.

. . .The district court held there are unique circumstances in this case which would make it fundamentally unfair for the Government to take the machines from their owners without first giving them the opportunity to pay the tax.

3. Use of Periods to Show Ellipsis

(a) Omission of Language at the Beginning of a Sentence. If, after deleting language at the beginning of a sentence, the remaining quoted language stands alone as a full sentence, capitalize the first letter and enclose it in brackets. Do not insert periods to indicate ellipsis. The fact that a lower case letter was changed to upper case indicates that words have been left out.

EXAMPLE: "[T]he Supreme Court shall have original jurisdiction."

(b) Omission of Language in the Middle of a Sentence. Indicate by the use of three periods separated by spaces.

EXAMPLE: "In case of the removal of the President..., the Vice President shall become President."

(c) Omission of Language at the End of a Sentence. Insert three periods to show ellipsis, followed by the period or other final punctuation.

EXAMPLE: "Congress shall make no law...."

> NOTE: The end punctuation is retained *after* the three ellipsis dots to make it clear that something in the last part of the sentence was left out. Compare the previous example with the following example.

(d) Omission of Language after the End of One Sentence and before the Beginning of the Next. Place the three periods indicating an ellipsis after the period at the end of the first sentence.

EXAMPLE: "The Senate shall have the sole Power to try all Impeachments.... [T]hey shall be on Oath or Affirmation."

> NOTE: Nothing was left out of the first sentence, so the period immediately followed "Impeachments" (no space between "Impeachments" and the period). You can tell by looking at the quote that something was left out at the beginning of the second sentence.

(e) Omission of Language in the Paragraph after the End of the Sentence. Do not indicate ellipsis. In the example just given in Section B.3(*d*), "Affirmation" was the last word of the quoted sentence but was not the last word in the paragraph. It is not necessary to show that in the original the quoted sentence was followed by more sentences.

(f) Phrases or Clauses. If the quoted matter is not used as a full sentence by itself, it is not necessary to indicate that words outside the quoted matter have been deleted.

EXAMPLE: As the court noted in <u>United States v. Morris</u>, "[d]irect observation is not essential to the existence of probable cause."

4. Use of Brackets to Show Textual Alterations

(a) Variation of Quoted Matter from the Original. You have already seen one use of brackets (changing upper to lower case or vice versa depending on the placement of quoted matter in a sentence). You may also use brackets to correct spelling, to alter the tense or number, to make the quoted material grammatically consistent with the rest of the text, or to insert explanatory material when the original language might be confusing if quoted out of context.

EXAMPLE:　The police report noted the observation of a "syringe left on [the top of the] auto seat."

EXAMPLE:　"The [statutory] intent is clear."

OR

"The statuary [sic: statutory] intent is clear."

NOTE: In the second example, the misspelling in the original was shown. This may be done purposely to lessen the credibility of an unfavorable opinion.

**Note that the Latin word "sic" is not italicized, in keeping with the Bluebook's "strong presumption" that Latin phrases frequently used in legal writing have fallen into common use.

EXAMPLE:　"Hence, to the extent that the claims [appellant] advances are not foreclosed by res judicata, it was clearly not an abuse of discretion for the Board to have refused to reopen the proceedings at this stage."

NOTE: In this example, "[appellant]" was substituted for the name of the party in the original. Even though some of the original language was omitted, you would not need an ellipsis to show the omission. The use of brackets itself conveys that fact.

EXAMPLE:　"The judicial review provision of the Act [8 U.S.C. § 1105a(a)(2)(1976)] provides that any petition for review shall be in the circuit in which the administrative proceedings were conducted."

NOTE: In this example, the bracketed material was an addition to the text, inserted for the sake of clarity.

EXAMPLE: In that case, the D.C. Circuit "concur[red] in the District Court's observation that Congress intended to strengthen the agency's remedial authority for assuring equal employment opportunity through the 1972 amendments."

> NOTE: In this example, the original language was "concurs."

(b) Deleting References to Footnotes in Text. If the original quotation taken from the text contains a reference to a footnote and you wish to delete it, at the end of the citation add the parenthetical explanation "(footnote omitted)."

EXAMPLE:

> In cases where the indictment itself charges possession, the defendant in a very real sense is revealed as a "person aggrieved by an unlawful search and seizure" upon a motion to suppress evidence prior to trial. Rule 41(c) should not be applied to allow the Government to deprive the defendant of standing to bring a motion to suppress by framing the indictment in general terms while prosecuting for possession.
>
> Jones v. United States, 362 U.S. 257, 264–65 (1960) (footnote omitted).

> NOTE: The original text contained a reference to footnote 1 immediately following the word "possession."

(c) Citation to Material Contained in a Footnote. If the quoted material itself is from the text of a footnote, that would be reflected in the citation as follows:

EXAMPLE: Hackley v. Roudebush, 520 F.2d 108, 136 n.110 (D.C. Cir. 1975).

(d) Addition of Emphasis. If you wish to underline certain words in the quote for emphasis, at the end of the citation add the explanation "(emphasis added)." In typewritten memos or briefs, each emphasized word is underlined continuously.

EXAMPLE: Section 4 of the Federal Water Power Act requires that proposed improvements in waterways be "desirable and

justified in the public interest for the purpose of improv-
ing or developing a waterway...." Act of June 10, 1920,
ch. 285, § 4(e), 16 U.S.C. § 797(e) (1976) (emphasis
added).

(e) Emphasis in the Original.   If emphasis appeared in the original, and you have left it intact, add the explanation "(emphasis in
original)."

(f) Citations Omitted.   It is often desirable to delete lengthy case
citations appearing in the text of the original quote. You may indicate
this omission by adding to the end of the quotation or citation "(citations omitted)." If, however, you wish to show that a court quoted
from or relied on an important decision for its holding, you may wish
to indicate this information as follows:

EXAMPLE: "Rule 41(e) applies the general principle that a party will
not be heard to claim a constitutional protection unless he
'belongs to the class for whose sake the constitutional protection is given.'" Jones v. United States, 362 U.S. 257,
261 (1960) (citing Hatch v. Reardon, 204 U.S. 152, 160
(1907)).

EXERCISE ⟦3⟧

Correct the following direct quotations as instructed. Unless otherwise indicated, all quotations are taken from Jones v. United States,
362 U.S. 257 (1960).

1. Locate the pinpoint cite:

   In order to qualify as a "person aggrieved by an unlawful search and
   seizure" one must have been a victim of a search or seizure, one against
   whom the search was directed, as distinguished from one who claims
   prejudice only through the use of evidence gathered as a consequence of
   a search or seizure directed at someone else.

   Jones v. United States, 362 U.S. 257, ⎯⎯ (1960).

2. Indicate whether the following quotations are to be run into the
text, or indented and single-spaced in block quotation form:

(*a*) The possession on the basis of which petitioner is to be and was convicted suffices to give him standing under any fair and rational conception of the requirements of Rule 41(e). _____

(*b*) A person aggrieved by an unlawful search and seizure may move the district court for the district in which the property was seized for the return of the property and to suppress for use as evidence anything so obtained on the ground that (1) the property was illegally seized without warrant, or (2) the warrant is insufficient on its face, or (3) the property seized is not that described in the warrant, or (4) there was not probable cause for believing the existence of the grounds on which the warrant was issued, or (5) the warrant was illegally executed. _____

3. In the following examples, indicate whether the first line of these block quotes should be further indented. (If so, place the ¶ symbol in front of the first word.)

(*a*) In the first count of a two-count indictment petitioner was charged with having "purchased, sold, dispensed, and distributed" narcotics in violation of 26 U.S.C. § 4704(a), that is, not in or from the "original stamped package." In the second count petitioner was charged under 21 U.S.C. § 174 with having "facilitated the concealment and sale of" the same narcotics, knowing them to have been imported illegally into the United States. Petitioner was found guilty on both counts and sentenced to seven years' imprisonment.

Jones v. United States, 362 U.S. 257, 258 (1960).

(*b*) Prior to trial petitioner duly moved to suppress the evidence obtained through the execution of the search warrant on the ground that the warrant had been issued without a showing of probable cause. The Government challenged petitioner's standing to make this motion because petitioner alleged neither ownership of the seized articles nor an interest in the apartment greater than that of an "invitee or guest."

Jones v. United States, 362 U.S. 257, 259 (1960).

4. In the following examples, words or paragraphs have been deleted from the original text. Indicate the omission appropriately, altering the capitalization if necessary.

(*a*) It is entirely proper to require of one who seeks to challenge the legality of a search as the basis for suppressing relevant evidence that he allege, and if the allegation be disputed that he establish, that he himself was the victim of an invasion of privacy.

Jones v. United States, 362 U.S. 257, 261 (1960).

(*b*) "It is not consonant with the amenities of the administration of criminal justice to sanction such squarely contradictory assertions of power by the Government." Jones v. United States, 362 U.S. 257, 263–64 (1960).

(*c*) "Both statutory provisions under which petitioner was prosecuted permit conviction upon proof of the defendant's possession of narcotics." Jones v. United States, 362 U.S. 257, 258 (1960).

(*d*) To establish "standing," Courts of Appeals have generally required that the movant claim either to have owned or possessed the seized property or to have had a substantial possessory interest in the premises searched. A defendant seeking to comply with what has been the conventional standing requirement has been forced to allege facts the proof of which would tend, if indeed not be sufficient, to convict him.

Jones v. United States, 362 U.S. 257, 261–62 (1960).

(*e*) The Government does not contend that only ownership of the premises may confer standing. It would draw distinctions among various classes of possessors, deeming some, such as 'guests' and 'invitees' with only the 'use' of the premises, to have too 'tenuous' an interest although concededly having 'some measure of control' through their 'temporary presence,' while conceding that others, who in a 'realistic sense, have dominion of the apartment' or who are 'domiciled' there, have standing.

Jones v. United States, 362 U.S. 257, 265 (1960).

(*f*) The District Court agreed to take evidence on the issue of petitioner's standing. Only petitioner gave evidence. On direct examination he testified that the apartment belonged to a friend, Evans, who had given him the use of it, and a key, with which petitioner had admitted himself on the day of the arrest.

In affirming petitioner's conviction the Court of Appeals agreed with the District Court that petitioner lacked standing, but proceeded to rule that even if it were to find that petitioner had standing, it would hold the evidence to have been lawfully received.

Jones v. United States, 362 U.S. 257, 259–60 (1960).

5. Correct the misspelled word by the use of brackets.

"The conferees intend that the transition from exemptions and requirements under present law to the amended law should not affect real estate already sold or leased as of the exective date of the amendments." House Conf. Rep. No. 706, 96th Cong., 1st Sess. 82 (1979), reprinted in 1979 U.S. Code Cong. & Ad. News 2402, 2441.

6. Indicate by brackets the statutory provisions under which petitioner was prosecuted.

> "Both statutory provisions under which petitioner was prosecuted permit conviction upon proof of the defendant's possession of narcotics ...." Jones v. United States, 362 U.S. 257, 258 (1960).

7. Indicate by brackets that the name "Didone" refers to the officer who applied for the warrant.

> "The sole evidence upon which the warrant was issued was an affidavit signed by Didone." Jones v. United States, 232 U.S. 257, 267 (1960).

8. Delete the reference to footnote 1 and add the appropriate parenthetical explanation.

> "Rule 41(e) should not be applied to allow the Government to deprive the defendant of standing to bring a motion to suppress by framing the indictment in general terms, while prosecuting for possession.[1]" Jones v. United States, 362 U.S. 257, 264–65 (1960).

9. The following quotation is itself taken from a footnote. Correct the citation accordingly.

> "The Government must... not permit a conviction to be obtained on the basis of possession, without the merits of a duly made motion to suppress having been considered." Jones v. United States, 362 U.S. 265 (1960).

10. Change the tense of "were" from *past* to *present* and indicate the change with brackets.

> The restrictions upon searches and seizures were obviously designed for protection against official invasion of privacy and the security of property. They are not exclusionary provisions against the admission of kinds of evidence deemed inherently unreliable or prejudicial.

Jones v. United States, 362 U.S. 257, 261 (1960).

11. Show that the underscored word was emphasized in the original text of the opinion.

> The suppression remedy for those owners in whose vehicles something is found and who are charged with crime is small consolation for all those owners <u>and</u> occupants whose privacy will be needlessly invaded by officers following mistaken hunches not rising to the level of prob-

able cause but operated on in the knowledge that someone in a crowded car will probably be unprotected if contraband or incriminating evidence happens to be found.

Rakas v. Illinois, 439 U.S. 128, 169 (1978) (White, J., dissenting).

12. Show that the underscored words were not emphasized in the original text of the opinion.

In order to qualify as a "person aggrieved by an unlawful search and seizure" one must have been a victim of a search or seizure, one against whom the search was directed, as distinguished from one who claims prejudice only through the use of evidence gathered as a consequence of a search or seizure directed at someone else.

Jones v. United States, 362 U.S. 257, 261 (1960).

13. Correct the errors in the following quotation, eliminate the citations appearing in the text, and indicate that you have done so.

[A] motion to suppress, under Rule 41 (c), must be made prior to trial, if the defendent then has knowledge of the grounds on which to base the motion. The Government argues that the defendant must establish his standing to suppress the evidence through affirmative allegations and may not wait to rest standing upon the government's case at the trial. This provisions of Rule 41 (e) ... is a crystalization of decisions of this Court requiring that procedure, and is designed to eliminate from the trial disputes over police conduct not immediately relevant to the question of guilt. See Nardone v. United States, 308 U.S. 338, 341–342; Segurola v. United States, 275 U.S. 106, 111–112; Agnello v. United States, 269 U.S. 20, 34; Adams v. New York, 192 U.S. 585.

Jones v. United States, 362 U.S. 257, 264 (1960).

C. SHEPARDIZING CASES

Shepard's is a research tool of multiple uses: it can be used to ascertain the disposition of a case on appeal, to identify where interim opinions in the same case have appeared, to locate parallel citations, to indicate how subsequent courts have viewed the opinion, to verify whether the opinion is still good law (i.e., has not been overruled, modified, or limited), or to obtain subsequent cases, law review articles, or annotations that mention the case.

For purposes of cite-checking, you will be concerned primarily with the disposition of a case on appeal (but you should also be alert to whether the case holding has been subsequently reversed or overruled). Certain aspects of the case history will also be found in Shepard's. Once you locate the information you need in Shepard's, you will verify it by going to the original source and then completing your citation accordingly.

1. Use of Shepard's

Following is a step-by-step guide to the use of Shepard's.

a. Go to the shelf and assemble, in order, all volumes of Shepard's covering the reporter in which the case you are Shepardizing appears.

b. Look on the spine of the volume of Shepard's to determine when it was compiled. If your case was published subsequent to the latest date on the spine, you need not consult that volume.

c. Go to the earliest volume of Shepard's applicable to your case. Consult that and all subsequent volumes and paperbound supplements in the series.

d. At the top of each page, and periodically down each column, you will find volume numbers printed in boldface type. Look for the volume number of the case you are Shepardizing.

e. In between volume numbers, you will find page numbers signifying the beginning of a new case. The page numbers are preceded and followed by dashes. After you have located the volume number of the case you are Shepardizing, look for the page number on which the case begins.

f. Under the page number, you will find a list of entries consisting of citations to other cases, articles and annotations. These entries will be broken down by jurisdiction (circuit or state court). To the left of certain entries will be lower case letters, signifying the history or treatment of a case.

g. Scan the entries under your case. You are interested only in entries preceded by the following letters:

s	(same case)	S	(superseded)
a	(affirmed)	v	(vacated)
D	(dismissed)	US cert den	(cert. denied)
m	(modified)	o	(overruled)
r	(reversed)		

h. If you find an entry showing that the case was subsequently disposed of as shown in the preceding list, copy the information given in Shepard's. Then, go to the shelf and find the volume that Shepard's has cited. Complete your citation accordingly. If you find that a case has been overruled, it should not be cited as currently in effect, for it is no longer good law.

2. Sample Search—Shepard's

You are Shepardizing the case of Shreeves v. United States, 395 A.2d 774, a 1978 case. You find that Shepard's Atlantic Reporter Citations consists of the following volumes:

Vol. 1, 1957 (covering 1 A.–124 A.2d)
1957–1958 Supplement to Vol. 1, 1957 (covering 1 A.–200 A.2d)
Vol. 2, Part 1, 1978 (covering 1 A.2d–200 A.2d)
Vol. 2, Part 2, 1978 (covering 201 A.2d–381 A.2d)
August 1981 Annual Supplement (gold paperbound, covering all volumes)
May 1982 Cumulative Supplement (red paperbound, covering all volumes)

The first volume of Shepard's in which your case (395 A.2d 774) appears is the August 1981 supplement. Therefore, check that volume and the red advance sheet published later.

Look for the pages having "Vol. 395" (2d series) at the top. Then skim down the columns to locate "-774-." Under that subheading you will find the following entries:[1]

US cert den	404A2d^{2}923	412A2d^{1}60
in 441US943	j411A2d651	Mo
f404A2d^{1}922	Me	605S$\overset{2}{w}$111

Without doing any further research, you know from this entry that the Supreme Court declined to take the case on appeal (cert. denied); that the holding in the case was followed ("f") in a subsequent volume of the Atlantic Reporter with respect to headnote 1 of the original case; that the case was cited in a dissenting opinion in another case reported in the Atlantic Reporter; that the case was also cited for a matter concerning headnote 2 of the original case; that a Maine case ("Me") appearing in volume 412 of A.2d also cited the Shreeves case, in a matter relating to headnote 1; and that a Missouri case appearing in 605 S.W.2d cited the case on page 111.

The only entry that concerns you for purposes of cite-checking is the first one: cert. denied, 441 U.S. 943. Go to the shelf, find 441 U.S., turn to page 943, find your case listed there, and note the year of decision (1979). Now complete your citation as follows:

EXAMPLE: Shreeves v. United States, 395 A.2d 774 (D.C. 1978), cert. denied, 441 U.S. 943 (1979).

If you are Shepardizing a case located in F. Supp. (federal trial court level), and you find the case affirmed in a later volume of F.2d (federal appellate level), you must now Shepardize the new case to see whether there was any disposition at the Supreme Court level.

If Shepard's indicates that an opinion was superseded ("S"), this means the opinion was rewritten by the same judge (usually with only slight variations from the original), and the later version is to be cited in place of the earlier.

If Shepard's indicates that an opinion concerns the same case ("s"), you will have to locate the subsequent opinion and determine whether it should be included in the prior or subsequent history of the citation. (See Section D of this chapter.)

Finally, if Shepard's merely indicates "cert. denied" or "appeal pending" at the time of publication without giving a citation, it probably means that the later disposition appeared too early to be included in a published source. You will have to track down recent dispositions of Supreme Court proceedings in the weekly loose-leaf published by BNA, U.S. Law Week. (See Section C.3, following.)

A word of caution about reversals ("r"): Generally, if a case is reversed on appeal, it may no longer be cited in a memorandum as good case law, because the original decision no longer holds. But, if only certain issues are raised on appeal, and the case is reversed on those grounds, any other issues in the original opinion are still intact and the case may still be usable to support propositions based on those grounds. In citing the case, you would indicate that it was reversed on other grounds, and include the subsequent appellate history in the citation. The appellate opinion itself will not spell it out; you will have to examine the case yourself to determine the basis of the reversal.

Also, if several issues are appealed in a complex case, a case may be reversed only in part on appeal. The subsequent history would then read aff'd in part and rev'd in part. Whether it can still be cited in the brief or memo depends on the status of the particular point for which the case is cited.

3. Use of U.S. Law Week

If you are trying to track down the disposition of a very recent Supreme Court case, you will have to search the weekly loose-leaf service, U.S. Law Week, Supreme Court edition.

Following is a step-by-step guide on how to use U.S. Law Week:

a. Be sure you are using the Supreme Court edition of U.S. Law Week, and not the General edition.

b. There will be three tabs in the current binder: Supreme Court Proceedings, Supreme Court Opinions and Supreme Court Index. The Index will contain a topical index, a table of cases, and a case status report (formerly called the Docket Number Table).

c. Turn to the table of cases and locate the Supreme Court docket number assigned to your case. Then consult the case status report section to find the numbers of the pages on which your case is discussed.

d. When a petition for certiorari is first filed with the Court, the case will be summarized in U.S. Law Week. It will be several weeks before the Court acts on the petition. (Only about one out of every hundred petitions is ultimately granted.)

e. If a petition is denied, the case can go no further. If a petition is granted, the case will later be argued before the Court and an opinion will be issued. A triangular-shaped symbol to the left of the index entry (△) indicates that an opinion has been published.

f. To be absolutely up to the minute, you must search each weekly issue of U.S. Law Week not covered by the index to determine the most recent action on a case. The format of each weekly issue will vary because actions taken by the court vary from one week to the next, but if you have the docket number, you should be able to locate any mention of your case quickly.

g. If you are verifying a U.S. Law Week cite that is several months old, chances are there is an official or unofficial citation now available. Once you ascertain the date of the decision, you can check the covers of the U.S. advance sheets to determine if the opinion has now been reported there. If not yet there, the opinion may already have been published in either the West's or Lawyer's Edition.

4. Sample Searches—U.S. Law Week—and How to Cite Your Findings

a. You have a 1978 Third Circuit case to Shepardize: Frissell v. Rizzo, 597 F.2d 840. The latest advance sheet of Shepard's indicates only "cert. denied."

(1) By checking the alphabetical table of cases, you will obtain the Supreme Court Docket No. (78–1890).

(2) By checking the Case Status Report, you learn that the case is summarized at page 3046 and that certiorari was denied, reported at page 3219.

(3) You may dispense with the first item and check the denial of certiorari. The date of decision is October 1, 1979 (the date given under Journal of Proceedings on page 3214).

(4) Checking the covers on advance sheets for U.S. Reports, you discover that decisions of October 1 through December 10, 1979, appear in volume 444, part 1. The Table of Cases gives you a citation to page 841. You may now complete the cite as follows: Frissell v. Rizzo, 597 F.2d 840 (3d Cir. 1978), cert. denied, 444 U.S. 841 (1979).

(5) If the advance sheet had not yet been printed, the last part of your cite would have read: cert. denied, 100 S. Ct. 82 (1979), or (if not yet published there) cert. denied, 48 U.S.L.W. 3219 (U.S. Oct. 1, 1979).

(6) If the petition for certiorari had not yet been acted upon, you would have checked the case summary and found that the petition had been filed on June 20, 1979, cited thus: petition for cert. filed, 48 U.S.L.W. 3046 (U.S. June 20, 1979) (No. 78–1890). This and other interim information will *not* be found in U.S. Reports or in West's Supreme Court Reporter. Note that in this example, the Supreme Court docket number was given, since a final decision in the application for certiorari was pending. This number is *not* included in a cert. denied cite, but *would* be included if certiorari were granted, because a final decision at the Supreme Court level would then be pending.

b. Following are further examples of how to cite the various stages of a case for which certiorari is ultimately granted.

Lewis v. United States, 591 F.2d 978 (4th Cir. 1979), petition for cert. filed, 48 U.S.L.W. 3066 (U.S. Apr. 18, 1979) (No. 78–1595).

Lewis v. United States, 591 F.2d 978 (4th Cir. 1979), cert. granted, 47 U.S.L.W. 3813 (U.S. June 19, 1979) (No 78–1595).

Lewis v. United States, 591 F.2d 978 (4th Cir. 1979), aff'd, 48 U.S.L.W. 4205 (U.S. Feb. 27, 1980).

Lewis v. United States, 591 F.2d 978 (4th Cir. 1979), aff'd, 100 S. Ct. 915 (1980).

Lewis v. United States, 591 F.2d 978 (4th Cir. 1979), aff'd, 445 U.S. 55 (1980).

How you complete the cite depends on the stage that the case has reached at the time you check your cite.

EXERCISE ④

Using Shepard's or other research tools described in the preceding chapter, Shepardize the following cases and complete or revise the citation where necessary.

1. In re Penn Central Securities Litigation, 416 F. Supp. 907 (E.D. Pa. 1976).

2. United States v. Hinds County School Board, 560 F.2d 1188 (5th Cir. 1977).

3. In re Namenson, 555 F.2d 1067 (1st Cir. 1977).

4. Tamari v. Bache Halsey Stuart, Inc., 619 F.2d 1196 (7th Cir. 1980), petition for cert. filed, 49 U.S.L.W. 3031 (U.S. July 24, 1980) (No. 80–110).

5. Intercounty Construction Corp. v. Walter, 44 L. Ed. 2d 643 (1975).

6. Alexander v. HUD, 99 S. Ct. 1572 (1979).

7. Lauritzen v. Chesapeake Bay Bridge & Tunnel District, 259 F. Supp. 633 (E.D. Va. 1966).

8. Daniel v. Waters, 399 F. Supp. 510 (M.D. Tenn. 1975).

9. In re Penn Central Securities Litigation, 347 F. Supp. 1327 (E.D. Pa. 1972).

10. Whitney v. California, 274 U.S. 357 (1927).

D. CITING PRIOR AND SUBSEQUENT HISTORY OF A CASE

Not every minute aspect of the case you are citing need be included in the citation but only certain relevant aspects of the case history. These are set forth in the Bluebook.

1. Prior History

(a) Give the prior history of a case only if significant to the point for which it is cited. (In practice, this is rarely necessary.) An example would be an appellate decision modifying an award of damages given by the lower court.

EXAMPLE: Zenith Radio Corp. v. Hazeltine Research, Inc., 395 U.S. 100 (1969), modifying 388 F.2d 25 (7th Cir. 1967).

(b) You will also give the prior history of a case if the given citation leads you to a Supreme Court memorandum decision (i.e., a disposition with no written opinion), to a table of affirmances appearing at the front of a reporter, or to similar abbreviated versions of the case.

EXAMPLE: Price v. Levers, 620 F.2d 289 (3d Cir.), aff'g 475 F. Supp. 937 (W.D. Pa. 1979).

> NOTE: It is preferable to cite to the meaningful opinion below, followed by the subsequent disposition in abbreviated form.

EXAMPLE: Price v. Levers, 475 F. Supp. 937 (W.D. Pa.), aff'd, 620 F.2d 289 (3d Cir. 1979).

(c) The prior history is given *after* the main case and is introduced and explained by italicized words, followed by the citation to the prior history. Do not repeat the name of the case, unless necessary because of a name change. (See Section D.3, following.)

EXAMPLE: Albrecht v. Herald Co., 452 F.2d 124 (8th Cir. 1971), aff'g in part and rev'g in part 321 F. Supp. 99 (E.D. Mo. 1970).

2. Subsequent History

(a) When citing a case in full, give the full subsequent history of a case on appeal, including whether it has been affirmed, reversed on other grounds, reversed in part, dismissed, vacated, modified, or certiorari denied or granted.

(b) If a case is remanded to a lower court, the history following remand will not be given unless it is relevant to the point for which the case is cited.

(c) It is likewise not necessary to state that a rehearing has been denied, unless it is relevant to the point being made (not likely unless you are discussing the need for a rehearing).

(d) If an appellate decision is later withdrawn by the deciding authority (such as an affirmance followed by reversal on rehearing), omit references to both events. The effect will be to leave the original decision intact.

(e) If you locate prior or subsequent decisions involving other issues in the case you are citing, you would rarely include these opinions in your citation unless they are directly relevant to the point you are citing.

EXAMPLE: Using Shepard's, you discover an interim opinion denying a party's motion to dismiss the case at the outset. The case proceeds to trial on the issue of whether the defendant's pricing scheme violates the Robinson–Patman Act. You would not include the preliminary opinion in the prior case history.

(f) The subsequent history is given after the main case and is similar in format to the prior history.

EXAMPLE: Albrecht v. Herald Co., 321 F. Supp. 99 (E.D. Mo. 1970), aff'd in part and rev'd in part, 452 F.2d 124 (8th Cir. 1971).

Note that in giving *subsequent* history, the explanatory phrase is set off by commas. In giving *prior* history, the second comma is omitted.

EXAMPLE (prior history): <u>Albrecht v. Herald Co.</u>, 452 F.2d 124 (8th Cir. 1979), <u>aff'g in part and rev'g in part</u> 321 F. Supp. 99 (E.D. Mo. 1970).

(g) A partial list of explanatory phrases is given on page 51 of the Bluebook. Note that the reason for a particular disposition will be given in certain situations for clarity:

<u>aff'd,</u>	<u>appeal dismissed,</u>
<u>aff'd on other grounds,</u>	<u>vacated as moot,</u>
<u>aff'g</u>	

The phrases that are followed by commas are appropriate for subsequent history. Those not followed by commas are used to cite prior history.

3. Different Case Name on Appeal

If litigation is protracted, and during the various appeal stages one of the parties has changed its name, become deceased, merged, dropped out of the litigation, or (as in the case of an elected or appointed official) been replaced, then the names of the parties will differ on appeal. Another transformation that may come about is that individual actions in complex litigation may later be consolidated.

BEFORE: <u>Saquoit v. Leesona Corp.</u>
AFTER: <u>In re Multidistrict Stretch Yarn Litigation.</u>

Your only hope of locating the correct citations to subsequent history in such cases is through <u>Shepard's</u>. If you try to locate a case with the aid of a case name index that is not kind enough to give a cross reference, you may become hopelessly confused. If <u>Shepard's</u> leads you to a table of orders denying certiorari, and you don't recognize the case you are looking for, check any references to the "case below" given in the case summaries in <u>U.S. Law Week</u>.

(a) When the name of a case differs in prior or subsequent history, the other name is generally given as follows:

(1) Prior history: <u>Pederi v. Isbrandtsen Co.</u>, 342 U.S. 590 (1952), <u>aff'g by an equally divided Court Isbrandtsen Co. v. United States</u>, 96 F. Supp. 883 (S.D.N.Y. 1951).

(2) Subsequent history—use "sub nom." form: Rosenfeld v. Lent, 353 F. Supp. (D. Mass.), aff'd sub nom. Healy v. Lent, 449 F.2d 232 (1st Cir. 1971).

(b) Different case names on appeal are *not* disclosed in three situations:

(1) *The names of the parties are merely reversed on appeal.* (Strictly speaking, this is not a name change. The losing party [defendant below] has become the appellant and is now named first).

(2) *The name is changed on a citation to* cert. denied. (Since no further decision using the new name will result, it is really not necessary to make an issue over the fact that the name has been changed.)

(3) *In the appeal of an administrative action to the court, the name of the private party remains the same.* (In agency actions, frequently only the name of the private party—the "respondent"—is given, it being understood that the agency has brought the action. On appeal, the agency itself is brought in as a party-defendant.) Thus, only if the name of the *private* party changes on appeal is the sub nom. form used.

EXAMPLES: Firth Carpet Co., 33 N.L.R.B. 191 (1941), enforced, 129 F.2d 633 (2d Cir. 1942).

John Q. Public, 34 N.L.R.B. 121 (1943), enforced sub nom. NLRB v. Bok, 139 F.2d 623 (2d Cir. 1944).

4. Which Level to Cite

Sometimes a decision is cited at the trial level, with information on the appellate opinion given in subsequent history, and at other times the appellate decision is cited directly, bypassing the lower court opinion. If the case has been heard by the Supreme Court, then the Supreme Court opinion is generally the only one cited to. Which is the appropriate level to cite to is a matter of judgment and may depend on the forum in which the case at hand is being argued, whether the trial court opinion contains a better exposition of the facts, whether the appellate opinion is brief and contains little quotable language, whether the trial court opinion has been thoroughly discredited on appeal, or whether the appellate decision represents a benchmark in the law. By properly following up on leads in Shepard's, you may discover a more appropriate level of citation. You may also correct internal inconsistencies within the brief or memorandum.

EXERCISE 5

The following examples may contain either too much history or not enough, or may not be in the proper form. Please correct. If the citation is correct as given, state "No change."

1. Penix v. Richardson, 468 F.2d 1259 (9th Cir. 1972), cert. denied, 36 L.Ed.2d 183 (1973), rehearing denied, 411 U.S. 978 (1973).

2. Goodbody & Co. v. Penjaska, 8 Mich. App. 64, 153 N.W.2d 665 (1967), cert. denied sub nom. Penjaska v. Goodbody & Co., 393 U.S. 16 (1968).

3. Platzman v. American Totalisator Co., 45 N.Y.2d 910, 383 N.E.2d 876, 411 N.Y.S.2d 230 (1978), aff'g, 57 App. Div. 2d 753, 57 App. Div. 2d 755, 394 N.Y.S.2d 412, 560 (1977).

4. Reyher v. Children's Television Workshop, 377 F. Supp. 411 (S.D.N.Y. 1974), complaint dismissed, 387 F. Supp. 869 (S.D.N.Y. 1975).

5. Marshall v. District of Columbia, 392 F. Supp. 1012 (D.D.C. 1975).

6. Perryman v. Washington, 405 U.S. 982 (1972), dismissing appeal sub nom. State v. Larsen, 4 Wash. App. 356, 481 P.2d 462 (1971).

7. United States v. Napoli, 530 F.2d 1198 (5th Cir.), cert. denied sub nom. Napoli v. United States, 429 U.S. 920 (1976).

E. USE OF SHORT FORMS

Although you must disclose all relevant prior and subsequent history the first time a case is cited, once the full citation is established, you may resort to an abbreviated form of citation. The acceptable short forms are id., "hereinafter," and merely a shortened form of the citation. These forms should not be used interchangeably but must be used only in situations specified in the Bluebook. In addition, supra and infra may be used to cite to other types of authorities.

1. Short Forms for Cases

Once a case has been named in text and cited in full, it is not necessary to use the full citation each time the case is mentioned again if it is clear from the context which case is being referred to. Subsequent references to the same case may be by the name of one of the parties, by an established popular name, by reference to the volume, reporter, and page number, or by any combination of these. If one of the parties is a government agency or representative, the name of the private party should be adopted as the short form. If a particular litigation has a long history of remands and relitigation, it may be desirable to refer to the various stages of the case as "I" and "II." The shortened name is appended to the full citation, as shown in the Zenith examples that follow.

EXAMPLES:　Full citation: Miranda v. Arizona, 384 U.S. 436, 450 (1966).
Short form: Miranda, 384 U.S. at 450.
Short form: 384 U.S. at 450.

Full citation: Zenith Radio Corp. v. Hazeltine Research, Inc., 395 U.S. 100 (1969) (Zenith I).
Short form: Zenith I.

Full citation: Zenith Radio Corp. v. Hazeltine Research, Inc., 401 U.S. 321 (1971) (Zenith II).
Short form: Zenith II.

You may also, if you wish, shorten the citation to the names of both parties.

EXAMPLE: Jackson v. Campbell.

An advantage to using the short form for citing cases is that you eliminate the need to repeat the case history.

EXAMPLE: First reference: Eisen v. Carlisle & Jacquelin, 370 F.2d 119 (2d Cir. 1966), cert. denied, 386 U.S. 1035 (1967).
Subsequent reference: Eisen, 370 F.2d at 120–21.

2. Short Forms for Statutes

The rules for short forms for statutes are similar to those for cases. Once a statute has been cited in full at the outset of a discussion, subsequent references may be to a popular name of the act and relevant section number.

EXAMPLE: First reference: The congressional declaration of national environmental policy is set forth in the National Environmental Policy Act of 1970, popularly known as NEPA. Pub. L. No. 91–190, 83 Stat. 852, 42 U.S.C. §§ 4321, 4331–4335, 4341–4347 (1976).

Subsequent reference: The Act established the Council on Environmental Quality to coordinate the efforts of governmental agencies in preparing Environmental Impact Statements. NEPA, § 4342.

Subsequent reference: 42 U.S.C. § 4342.

3. Use of Id.

Id. is a Latin abbreviation for a word meaning "in the same place." It may be used as a short form for any kind of authority, including cases and statutes, when citing to the immediately preceding authority.

EXAMPLE: In addition to requiring a court to have general jurisdiction before immunity attaches, there is persuasive authority that a court, at least when ordering the extreme remedy of sterilization, must have specific legislative or common-law authority to do so. See, e.g., Sparkman v. McFarlin, 552 F.2d 172, 175–76 (7th Cir. 1977). In that case, the court found that a state judge who ordered the permanent sterilization of a young woman was susceptible to suit for civil damages. Id. at 176.

NOTE: In this example, if there had been intervening authorities between the first and subsequent references to the Sparkman case, "id." would no longer be appropriate, and the subsequent reference to Sparkman would be as follows:

EXAMPLE: See, e.g., Sparkman v. McFarlin, 552 F.2d 172, 175–76 (7th Cir. 1977); Wade v. Bethesda Hospital, 337 F. Supp. 671, 673–74 (S.D. Ohio 1971). In Sparkman, the court found that a state judge who ordered the permanent sterilization of a young woman was susceptible to suit for civil damages. 552 F.2d at 176.

If the subsequent citation is to the same page or section number as the first citation, simply cite id. If, however, the subsequent citation varies in any particular from the first citation, indicate the changed page or section number as follows:

EXAMPLE: First citation: Public Vessels Act of 1925, 46 U.S.C §§ 781–90 (1976).
Subsequent reference: Id. § 783.

Do *not* use id. if the first citation is to a subdivision of a source and the subsequent citation is to the authority as a whole. Simply repeat the entire citation, omitting reference to the subdivision, as follows:

EXAMPLE: First citation: 6 J. Moore, W. Taggart & J. Wicker, Moore's Federal Practice ¶ 56.07, at 56–116 (2d ed. 1981).
Subsequent citation: See generally J. Moore, W. Taggart & J. Wicker, Moore's Federal Practice (2d ed. 1981).

If the authority is a case that requires parallel citations, use the following form:

EXAMPLE: First citation: Kansas City Southern Railway v. Leinen, 144 Ark. 454, 223 S.W. 1 (1920).
Subsequent citation: 144 Ark. at 455, 233 S.W. at 2.
Subsequent citation (immediately following): Id. at 456, 223 S.W. at 3.

4. Use of Supra and Infra

Supra and infra are Latin words for "above" and "below." Thus, once you have cited to an authority in full, subsequent references to the same authority may be made by the use of supra (if id. is not appropriate). Note that supra and infra should *not* be used in reference to cases and statutes. Instead, use the short forms given previously.

EXAMPLE: First reference (appearing on page 10 of a brief): 4 L. Loss, Securities Regulation 2203 (2d ed. Supp. 1969).
Subsequent reference: 4 L. Loss, supra p. 10, at 2205.

If the first reference appeared in a footnote, then the subsequent reference should include reference to the footnote number.

EXAMPLE: 4 L. Loss, <u>supra</u> note 5, at 2205.

If an authority appears more than once within a single footnote, in addition to other authorities, subsequent references to the earlier authority within that footnote need not include the footnote number.

EXAMPLE: [1]The rules of practice of the Civil Aeronautics Board state that it is improper for any person interested in the outcome of the case to give statements to the press calculated to influence the Board's judgment in the case. 4 M. Volz, <u>West's Federal Practice Manual</u> § 4699 (2d ed. 1970). The purpose of this provision was to strengthen the prohibition against ex parte communications with Board members. United Airlines v. CAB, 281 F.2d 53 (D.C. Cir. 1960). Any person found by the Board to have engaged in unethical or improper professional conduct may be disqualified by the Board. 4 M. Volz, <u>supra</u>, § 4701.

The Bluebook specifies the appropriate use of <u>supra</u>, which varies according to the type of authority being cited:

(a) Works by a named author: Cite by author.

EXAMPLE: 4 M. Volz, <u>supra</u> p. 6, § 4701.

(b) Unsigned works: Cite by title.

EXAMPLE: <u>Symposium</u>, <u>supra</u> note 13, at 289.

(c) Student-written materials (such as student notes): Cite by designation.

EXAMPLE: Note, <u>supra</u> note 5, at 97.

The <u>supra</u> citation should include the page of the text or footnote in which the authority was first cited, followed by reference to volume, page, paragraph, or section number of the authority being cited. Note that citation to page numbers (but not paragraph or section numbers) is preceded by "at."

Supra (and infra) may also be used to direct the reader to groups of authorities appearing elsewhere in the brief, memorandum, or law review article.

**EXAMPLE: For a discussion of federal securities registration requirements, see infra p. 41.
**EXAMPLE: See generally authorities cited supra note 22.

> NOTE: Although it is appropriate to use infra in the manner illustrated in these examples (cross references to related authorities elsewhere in the brief), it is not proper to use infra in the first citation in lieu of citing to an authority in full.

WRONG: First reference: Hearings on Treatment of Women, infra at 11.

RIGHT: First reference: Treatment of Women Under Social Security: Hearings Before the Task Force on Social Security and Women of the House Subcomm. on Retirement Income and Employment and the House Select Comm. on Aging, 96th Cong., 1st Sess. 40 (1979) [hereinafter cited as Hearings on Treatment of Women].
Subsequent reference: Hearings on Treatment of Women, supra p. 3, at 15.

Note that in using any of the short forms discussed in this chapter the authority itself will retain the same typeface as it would in a full citation.

5. Use of "Hereinafter"

The use of "hereinafter" is appropriate to establish a special shortened form for certain authorities to be cited several times. The "hereinafter" form is established in the very first citation to the authority, enclosed in brackets as shown in the following.

EXAMPLE: First reference: Household Goods Transportation Act of 1979: Hearings on S. 1798 Before the S. Comm. on Commerce, Science and Transportation, 96th Cong., 1st Sess. 245 (1979) [hereinafter cited as Transportation Hearings].

There are no special rules for the exact short form to be used; what is appropriate may depend on other sources cited throughout the brief which may be confusingly similar.

Once a "hereinafter" form has been established, the shortened form must be used in all subsequent references, followed by a comma and the world supra.

EXAMPLE: Subsequent reference: Transportation Hearings, supra p. 17, at 221.

If the first reference appeared in a footnote, then the subsequent reference should include a reference to the footnote as follows:

EXAMPLE: Subsequent reference: Transportation Hearings, supra note 3, at 221.

> NOTE: The use of "hereinafter" is optional. Do *not* use "hereinafter" when the simple supra form would be adequate.

As in the case of supra and infra, "hereinafter" is not generally used to refer to cases, statutes, or similar material (such as rules and regulations). However, exceptional circumstances occasionally do exist, such as establishing a special form for cases with unwieldly names.

EXAMPLE: In re Multidistrict Private Civil Treble Damage Antitrust Litigation Involving Motor Vehicle Air Pollution Control Equipment, 52 F.R.D. 398 (C.D. Cal. 1970) [hereinafter cited as Air Pollution Control Case].

EXERCISE 6

The following examples contain a full citation to the given authority. You are to give a subsequent reference, using the appropriate short form. Unless stated otherwise, assume that the subsequent reference does not immediately follow the first reference.

1. Stegall v. United States, 153 F. Supp. 844, 847 (W.D. Ky. 1957), aff'd, 259 F.2d 83 (6th Cir. 1958).
Subsequent reference: page 850, 153 F. Supp.

2. Eisen v. Carlisle & Jacquelin, 391 F.2d 555 (2d Cir. 1968).
Eisen v. Carlisle & Jacquelin, 479 F.2d 1105 (2d Cir. 1973).
Subsequent reference: 479 F.2d, page 1110.
3. Deaton v. Vise, 186 Tenn. 364, 210 S.W.2d 665 (1948).
Subsequent reference: page 365, Tenn.; page 666, S.W.2d.
4. Truth in Lending Act § 130(a), 15 U.S.C. § 1640(a) (Supp. IV, 1980).
Subsequent reference (immediately following): section 130(a)(2), 15 U.S.C. § 1640(a)(2).
5. Doe v. Poelker, 515 F.2d 541 (8th Cir. 1975), cert. denied, 428 U.S. 909 (1976).
Subsequent reference: page 548, F.2d.
6. Same case, with subsequent reference immediately following.
7. The Wunderlich Act, 41 U.S.C. §§ 321–322 (1976).
Subsequent reference (immediately following): section 322.
8. Sloan v. Jones, 192 Tenn. 400, 241 S.W.2d 506 (1951).
Subsequent reference (immediately following): page 407, 192 Tenn.; page 510, 241 S.W.2d.
9. 11 C. Wright & C. Miller, Federal Practice and Procedure § 2948, at 440 (1973).
Subsequent reference (immediately following): § 2948, page 439.
10. Human Rights and the Phenomenon of Disappearances: Hearings Before the Subcomm. on Internal Organizations of the House Comm. on Foreign Affairs, 96th Cong., 1st Sess. 175 (1979) [hereinafter cited as Human Rights Hearings].
Subsequent reference: page 388.

3 | *How to Cite Cases*

This chapter describes how to properly cite court cases and administrative proceedings in text and in footnotes and sets forth the rules for citing each element of the citation in accordance with the Bluebook: case name, reporter, court, jurisdiction, and date of decision. In state cases, the correct forms for parallel citation are demonstrated.

As you have seen, citations to cases consist of several components: the case name, the volume and name of the reporter or reporters in which it appears, the name of the court or agency rendering the decision, and the date of decision. The full citation may also include an introductory signal, the prior and subsequent history of a case, and parentheticals indicating the weight of authority or explaining the holding. This chapter will explain how to cite to a case from the name to the date of decision. It will explain the rules to be applied depending on whether the citation appears in the text or in a footnote.

NOTE: This chapter and succeeding chapters contain a number of complex rules you are not likely to encounter often. To assist you in concentrating on those items most useful to you, the more esoteric items are marked with an asterisk. The exercises will concentrate on the more common citation problems.

A. CASE NAMES IN TEXT

The starting point in citing the name of a case is the name that appears at the beginning of the opinion in the official report. The rules here are designed to eliminate superfluous information from the citation. If no name appears in the official report, use a popular name or cite it simply as "Judgment of [full date]."

In the text of a typewritten brief or law review article, the case name is underlined with an unbroken line. Do not underline the comma following the case name. If the word processing system with which you are working makes this approach infeasible, you may disregard this rule and underline each word separately.

Following is a step-by-step guide to citing cases in the text of a memorandum or brief.

1. Always retain in full the first word in each party's name. Note that this rule applies to both plaintiff and defendant.

WRONG: Irwin v. U.S.
RIGHT: Irwin v. United States.

2. Many reported cases represent the consolidation of two or more actions. Use only the first case listed; ignore the consolidated actions.

WRONG: Marathon Oil Co. v. EPA, Shell Oil Co. v. EPA.
RIGHT: Marathon Oil Co. v. EPA.

3. Many cases also list multiple parties at the beginning of the reported opinion (often in less conspicuous typeface). In citing the case, omit all parties other than the first party listed on each side.

WRONG: Marathon Oil Co., Union Oil Co. of California, Atlantic
        Richfield Co., and Mobil Oil Corp. v. EPA.
RIGHT: Marathon Oil Co. v. EPA.

4. In cases involving a relator (that is, an attorney general or other official filing a case on behalf of a private party), the

name of the relator as well as that of the private party is retained in the case name. The relationship between the relator
and the party in interest is indicated by the phrase <u>ex rel</u>.

WRONG: United States v. Casey.
RIGHT: United States ex rel. TVA v. Casey.

5. If one of the parties is a partnership, do not omit any portion of
the partnership name.

WRONG: Tanzer v. Merrill, Lynch.
RIGHT: Tanzer v. Merrill, Lynch, Pierce, Fenner & Smith, Inc.

6. Omit alternative names given for any party, such as a trade
name under which the party conducts business.

WRONG: Donald R. Gumm and Katherine Gumm, d/b/a Mineral
Springs Motel, Katharine Gumm and General Insurance
Co. of America v. National Homes Acceptance Corp.
RIGHT: Gumm v. National Homes Acceptance Corp.

7. Phrases or party names that would aid in identifying the case
may be indicated in parentheses after the formal name.

EXAMPLE: National Woodworking Manufacturers Association v.
NLRB (Sand Door).

8. Bankruptcy proceedings brought by or against a trustee in
bankruptcy should be cited as adversary cases, with the name
of the bankruptcy proceeding given parenthetically.

EXAMPLE: Mose v. O.M. Scott & Sons (In re Riedl).

9. Abbreviate such phrases as "on the relation of," "for the use
of," "on behalf of," and similar expressions to <u>ex rel</u>.

WRONG: Tri-State Corp. v. Alabama on the relation of Richmond
F. Flowers.
RIGHT: Tri-State Corp. v. Alabama ex rel. Flowers.

10. Abbreviate "in the matter of," "petition of," "application of," and similar expressions to <u>in re</u>, provided only one party is named.

WRONG: <u>In the matter of Trimble Company.</u>
RIGHT: <u>In re Trimble Co.</u>

11. When adversary parties are named, omit procedural phrases such as <u>in re</u>.

WRONG: <u>In re Ellman v. Tusk.</u>
RIGHT: <u>Ellman v. Tusk.</u>

12. "Estate of" and "Will of" are not considered procedural phrases, but are part of the case name. Do not omit these terms:

WRONG: <u>In re Smythe.</u>
RIGHT: <u>In re Will of Smythe.</u>

13. When the full name of a party can be abbreviated to widely recognized initials (such as the initials of a government agency), do so. This is an exception to the requirement that the first word in a party name always be spelled out. When abbreviating, omit periods after the initials.

WRONG: <u>R.A. Holman & Co. v. Securities & Exchange Commission.</u>
WRONG: <u>R.A. Holman & Co. v. S.E.C.</u>
RIGHT: <u>R.A. Holman & Co. v. SEC.</u>

NOTE: "United States" is never abbreviated in a case name.

14. The only other abbreviations permitted in case names cited in the text are the following: Co., Corp., Inc., Ltd., No., and "&" (ampersand symbol, used in place of "and").

EXAMPLE: <u>Lone Star Cement Co. v. FTC.</u>

15. Generally, if "The" appears as the first word of a party name, it is omitted.

WRONG: <u>The Hannahville Indian Community v. United States.</u>
RIGHT: <u>Hannahville Indian Community v. United States.</u>

16. EXCEPTION: "The" is *retained* as the first word of a case name when referring to the object of an in rem action, that is, an action involving the seizure of property. The object may be a vessel, a piece of land, merchandise seized by the government, or the like. If "The" is not part of the case name, do not add it.

EXAMPLE: <u>The Innerton.</u>

17. EXCEPTION: "The" is *retained* in the case name if the named party is "The King" or "The Queen."

18. EXCEPTION: Certain established popular names begin with the word "The." When citing to such a case, "The" is *retained.*

EXAMPLE: <u>The Civil Rights Cases.</u>

19. Omit descriptive terms used to indicate the status or title of a named party, such as "plaintiff," "defendant," "administrator," "appellee," "executor," "licensee," and "trustee."

WRONG: <u>Lehigh Valley Railroad, Libellant v. The Tug Blackjack 21, Respondent.</u>
RIGHT: <u>Lehigh Valley Railroad v. The Tug Blackjack 21.</u>

WRONG: <u>Board of Education, Troy Community Consolidated School District No. 30C v. Will County Board of School Trustees.</u>
RIGHT: <u>Board of Education v. Will County Board of School Trustees.</u>

NOTE: In the above example, "Trustees" is part of the name of the entity, rather than an added descriptive term.

20. Generally drop geographical terms such as "State of," "Commonwealth of," and "People of" appearing at the beginning of a case name.

WRONG: State of California v. United States.
RIGHT: California v. United States.

21. EXCEPTION: When a case is brought in the court of a particular state, and the named state is one of the parties, the rule is reversed. Retain the geographical term "State," "Commonwealth," or "People," and drop the remaining words in the party name.

WRONG: State of Maine v. Robinson, 403 A.2d 1201 (Me. 1980).
WRONG: Maine v. Robinson, 403 A.2d 1201 (Me. 1980).
RIGHT: State v. Robinson, 403 A.2d 1201 (Me. 1980).

> HINT: When the full citation indicates that the action was brought in a state court, it is not necessary to repeat the name of the state in the case name.

22. The rules concerning phrases of location are tricky. Watch out for such phrases as "City of," "County of," and similar expressions. If they appear at the *beginning of* a party name, keep them in.

EXAMPLE: City of Chicago v. FPC.

23. If they appear in the *middle* of a party name, leave them out.

WRONG: Mayor of City of Baltimore v. Crown, Cork & Seal Co.
RIGHT: Mayor of Baltimore v. Crown, Cork & Seal Co.

24. If a prepositional phrase of location is *not* introduced by a phrase such as "City of" or "Village of," omit the phrase altogether, *unless to do so would leave only one* word in the name of a party.

WRONG: Mayfield v. First National Bank of Chattanooga, Tennessee.
RIGHT: Mayfield v. First National Bank. (Delete "of Chattanooga, Tennessee.")

WRONG: Bank v. Fidelity & Casualty Co. of New York.
RIGHT: Bank of Altenburg v. Fidelity & Casualty Co. (Don't leave
              "Bank" by itself.)

When dealing with corporate names, special circumstances may
justify varying from this rule. For example, the name of a corporation
may include a geographical term that distinguishes the company from
its counterparts in other jurisdictions (such as Standard Oil of Indiana or Standard Oil of New Jersey). In such a case, the geographical
term should be retained for the sake of integrity.

   25. Always *include* all designations of national or continental areas
        (except in union names).

EXAMPLE: Bank of America v. Seville. (Retain "of America.")

   26. EXCEPTION: Omit "of America" whenever it appears after
        "United States."

WRONG: United States of America v. Marshall.
RIGHT: United States v. Marshall.

   27. Include *all* geographical designations of whatever level that are
        not introduced by a preposition.

EXAMPLE: Phoenix Assurance Co. v. Franklin Brass Co. (Retain
              "Phoenix.")

   28. A distinction is made between names of individuals and names
        of companies. Individuals are cited by their last name only.
        (Omit first names and initials.) Business names are retained in
        full.

EXAMPLE: Individual name: United States v. Miller.
              Business name: L.N. Jackson & Co. v. Lorentzen.

   29. In business names, if the company name includes a term such
        as "Co.," "Bros," or "Ass'n" (so that the name of the party
        obviously refers to a business and not an individual), omit the
        final "Inc." or "Ltd."

WRONG: <u>Wahl v. Carrier Manufacturing Co., Inc.</u>
RIGHT: <u>Wahl v. Carrier Manufacturing Co.</u>

**30. The Bluebook rules for citing union names are designed to simplify the citation as much as possible.

(*a*) In citing union names, include only the name of the smallest grass roots unit. Omit regional or national affiliates, as well as all prepositional phrases of location.

WRONG: <u>Blake Construction Co. v. Laborers' International Union of North America, AFL-CIO.</u>
RIGHT: <u>Blake Construction Co. v. Laborers' International Union.</u>

(*b*) In citing the craft or industry, retain the first full designation and drop reference to all others.

WRONG: <u>Local 174, Teamsters, Chauffeurs, Warehousemen & Helpers of America v. Lucas Floor Co.</u>
RIGHT: <u>Local 174, Teamsters v. Lucas Floor Co.</u>

(*c*) A widely recognized abbreviation of the union name may be used.

EXAMPLE: <u>United States Steel Corp. v. UMW.</u>

   31. If the Commissioner of Internal Revenue (CIR) is cited as a party, reduce the party name to Commissioner.

   32. If the name of a party is a federal agency, such as U.S. Department of Transportation or United States Environmental Protection Agency, you may omit the reference to "United States" from the case name.

EXAMPLE: <u>Department of Justice v. Slater.</u>

EXERCISE 1

Using the rules cited in the Bluebook as a guide, correct the following case name citations. Assume that the citation is made in text. If the citation is correct as given, state "No change."

1. Tom W. Carpenter Equipment Co. v. GE Credit Corp.
2. Indiana State Employees Association, Inc. v. Richard A. Boehning.
3. U.S. v. 11 Acres of Land, More or Less, Situate in City of Port Washington, Nassau County, N.Y.
4. C.I.R. v. Weinrich's Estate.
5. Petition of Committee of Censors of the City of Philadelphia Bar Association.
6. Commonwealth of Kentucky, for Use and Benefit of Kern v. Md. Casualty Co. of Baltimore, Maryland [U.S. district court case].
7. Commonwealth of Pa. ex rel. Toliver v. Ashe [Pa. state court case].
8. Connecticut Fire Insurance Co. v. Reliance Insurance Co. of Madison, Wisconsin.
9. The Toledo.
10. Town of Bristol v. U.S. for & on behalf of the Small Business Administration.

B. CASE NAMES IN LAW REVIEW FOOTNOTES

There are a few minor but important differences to keep in mind in citing cases appearing in law review footnotes. The first class of rules pertains to abbreviations.

1. Abbreviations

(a) As in cases cited in text, always spell out the first word of a name of a party. Otherwise, use the abbreviations listed on pages 41–42 of the Bluebook. Note that the abbreviations will utilize either a period or an apostrophe but not both.

EXAMPLE: Committee is abbreviated Comm. Comm'n is the abbreviated form for Commission.

(b) The inside back cover of the Bluebook contains a list of abbreviations for states, Canadian provinces, and foreign countries.

EXAMPLE: California is abbreviated Cal.

(c) It is permissible to abbreviate other words of eight letters or more, using a recognizable designation, but only if substantial space

will be saved (as would occur when a case is cited numerous times within a brief or memorandum).

EXAMPLE: Secretary may be abbreviated Sec'y.

(d) Form plurals by inserting an "s" inside the period. If no period is used in the singular form, simply add "s."

EXAMPLE: Co., Cos., Dep't, Dep'ts.

> NOTE: The list of abbreviations in the Bluebook may indicate that the same form is to be used for singulars and plurals. For that reason, you should always consult the Bluebook first.

EXERCISE 2

Referring to the Bluebook, further correct the case name citations given in Exercise 1 as though the cases were cited in a footnote. If the citation is correct as given, state "No change." For convenience, the list is repeated here.

1. Tom W. Carpenter Equipment Co. v. GE Credit Corp.
2. Indiana State Employees Association, Inc. v. Richard A. Boehning.
3. U.S. v. 11 Acres of Land, More or Less, Situate in City of Port Washington, Nassau County, N.Y.
4. C.I.R. v. Weinrich's Estate.
5. Petition of Committee of Censors of the City of Philadelphia Bar Association.
6. Commonwealth of Kentucky, for Use and Benefit of Kern v. Md. Casualty Co. of Baltimore, Maryland [U.S. district court case].
7. Commonwealth of Pa. ex rel. Toliver v. Ashe [Pa. state court case].
8. Connecticut Fire Insurance Co. v. Reliance Insurance Co. of Madison, Wisconsin.
9. The Toledo.
10. Town of Bristol v. U.S. for & on behalf of the Small Business Administration.

2. Special Rules—Railroads

Cases in which one of the parties is a railroad have special rules when the citation appears in a law review footnote.

(a) Always spell out the first word in the name in full.

EXAMPLE: Minneapolis, N&S Ry. v. Kelm.

(b) If the first word in the party's name is a geographical term consisting of two or more words, spell out the geographical term in full.

EXAMPLE: New York Cent. & H.R.R. v. ICC.

(c) Geographical words other than the first word in a party name should be abbreviated to the initial letter or to recognized abbreviations.

EXAMPLE: Baltimore & O. Ry. v. Domestic Hardwoods.

(d) As in textual citations, omit the word "Co." when referring to a railroad company (unless the name in the official report is simply "Railroad Company").

WRONG: Chicago, R.I. & R.R. Co. v Gill.
RIGHT: Chicago, R.I. & R.R. v. Gill.

3. Typeface

Regarding the typeface of case names, the Bluebook makes a distinction between citations given in the text of the writing, citations given in law review footnotes, and discussions of cases appearing in law review footnotes. (Remember that this guide uses underlines to show words italicized in print.)

(a) Case Names in Text. The rules for citing case names in text are simple. Italicize all case names, including the "v." and any procedural phrases. In typed materials, the case name will be underlined instead of italicized.

(b) Case Names in Law Review Footnotes—Citations. If a full citation to a case is given in a footnote, the "in-text" rule is reversed:

No part of the case name is italicized. It appears in regular roman type. Procedural phrases such as in re, however, are always italicized.

EXAMPLE: Bradford v. United States, 413 F.2d 467 (5th Cir. 1969).

(c) Case Names in Law Review Footnotes—Discussions. If a law review footnote contains discussions of cases, the case name may or may not be italicized, depending on the nature of the reference.

(1) If a case in a law review footnote is cited in full, use regular roman type (no italics).

(2) In law review footnotes as well as text, the first time a case is cited it is cited in full. Subsequently, it may be cited using the short form shown in the following example.

EXAMPLE: Bradford v. United States, 413 F.2d at 470.

If the short form includes the full name of the case, the typeface is still regular roman.

(3) If the short form includes the name of only one of the parties, the name is italicized.

EXAMPLE: The Court in Seldin, 422 U.S. at 516, held that the Home
          Builders Association had no standing to claim damages
          on its own behalf.

(4) If a case is mentioned by name only (no citation), it is also italicized.

EXAMPLE: In Warth v. Seldin, plaintiffs challenged a municipal zon-
          ing ordinance allegedly designed to exclude low- and
          middle-income people from a township.

Thus, the rules can be summarized as follows:

Full citations and short forms including the full name of the case, volume, and page number—regular typeface.

Reference to cases by name only or by using only one of the party names—italics.

Thus, in law review footnotes, italics are used generally for less-than-full citations.

EXERCISE 3

Review the case names contained in the following footnote. Underline where appropriate. If the typeface is to remain regular roman, put a check above the case name.

1. Cross Key, 372 So. 2d at 918. Although a Florida appellate court in Albrecht v. Department of Envt'l Regulation, 353 So. 2d 883, 887 (Fla. Dist. Ct. App. 1978), has stated that the 1974 Florida Administrative Procedure Act provides an "array of procedural safeguards [and] has lessened the need for strict statutory standards in the delegation of power to administrative agencies," that position has not been followed by the Florida Supreme Court. At one time, it seemed that then Justice (now Chief Justice) England of the Florida Supreme Court was about to adopt the modern position:

> In summary, I conceive that the Legislature has lawfully delegated to the executive branch the enforcement of its announced policy in this area. There is no abuse of that delegation so long as the class of prohibited acts are more specifically defined by prospective administrative action to which the Administrative Procedure Act applies.

Department of Legal Affairs v. Rogers, 329 So. 2d 257, 269 (Fla. 1976) (England, J., concurring). However, Chief Justice England's concurring opinion in Cross Key is diametrically opposed to the Davis view:

> Justice Sundberg [the author of the Askew v. Cross Key Waterways opinion] has revitalized a vastly more important doctrine—one that guarantees that Florida's government will continue to operate only by consent of the governed. He is saying, quite simply, that whatever may be the governmental predilections elsewhere, in Florida no person in one branch of our government may by accident or by assignment act in a role assigned by the Constitution to persons in another branch.

372 So. 2d at 925. Then, however, in Department of Business Regulation v. National Manufactured Hous. Fed'n, 370 So. 2d 1132, 1137 (Fla. 1979), the Chief Justice concurred in the result only. Although all this may lead one to speculate about the Chief Justice's position, the recent cases indicate that the position of the Florida Supreme Court cannot be questioned. See, e.g., Florida Home Builders Ass'n v. Division of Labor, 367 So. 2d 219 (Fla. 1979).[1]

C. NAMES OF ADMINISTRATIVE CASES AND ARBITRATIONS

The rules given in the preceding sections have focused on court cases. Cases brought by an administrative agency (such as the Federal Trade Commission) have a slightly different format.

Generally, administrative cases are brought in the name of the agency and decided before an administrative law judge of that agency. There may be an appellate review procedure before all commissioners of the agency. Information identifying the agency will appear elsewhere in the citation. Therefore, only the private party against whom the proceeding is brought (the respondent) will be mentioned in the case name.

1. Cite administrative actions by the full reported name of the first-listed private party. All procedural phrases (such as "in the matter of") are omitted.

EXAMPLE: Certified Building Products, Inc.

2. Occasionally, an agency will wage an industrywide battle, and the result will be several consolidated cases known by a subject-matter title.

EXAMPLE: Seven-Eleven Franchise Antitrust Litigation.

3. Decisions of the Internal Revenue Service are tried in the Tax Court and Board of Tax Appeals. They are treated as a court case, with "Commissioner" given as the nonprivate party.

EXAMPLE: Commissioner v. Phillips.

Note that agency decisions may be appealed in the courts, with the agency being named as a party. The case then becomes a court case and is treated accordingly. The determining factor is the forum in which the case is brought.

4. Arbitrations are treated either as court cases or as administrative actions, depending on whether one or two parties are named.

EXAMPLES: <u>Chemineer, Inc.</u> (treat as administrative action).
<u>Southern Pacific Co. v. Bishop</u> (treat as court case).

**In all arbitration citations, the name of the arbitrator should be given parenthetically.

EXAMPLE: <u>Amax, Inc.</u>, 76 Lab. Arb. (BNA) 607 (1981) (Moats, Arb.).

EXAMPLE: <u>Department of Transportation v. PATCO</u>, [1979–1980 Arbitrations] Fed. Lab. Rel. Rep. ¶ 2-1146 (1979) (Duff, Arb.).

EXERCISE 4

The following cases all involve an administrative agency or a matter under arbitration. Give the proper case name citation, depending on whether it is a court case or administrative proceeding. The forum is indicated in brackets.

1. <u>FPC v. Amerada Petroleum Corp.</u> [Supreme Court].
2. <u>NLRB v. Axton Candy & Tobacco Co.</u> [N.L.R.B.].
3. <u>Environmental Defense Fund, Inc. v. HEW</u> [D.C. Cir.].
4. <u>R.T. Myers and Emily S. Myers</u> [Tax Court].
5. <u>Atlanta & St. Andrews Bay Ry. Co.</u> [Labor Arbitration].

D. REPORTERS

Information regarding the reporter (that is, the publication in which the opinion is printed) consists of three parts: the volume number, the name of the reporter, and the page number on which the case begins. Each part is separated by a space.

EXAMPLE: 352 F.2d 80.

1. Name of Reporter

The name of the reporter is given in regular roman type, using the appropriate abbreviated form listed in the Bluebook on pages 133–35 (federal courts), 135–36 (federal agencies), and 136–76 (state courts).

2. Name of Editor

Older reporters for U.S. Supreme Court opinions and some state reports were often named after their editors rather than the courts in which the opinion was issued. Some of these were later combined into a series named by jurisdiction, so that a special citation form must be used.

EXAMPLE: Cooley v. Board of Wardens, 53 U.S. (12 How.) 299 (1851).

Note that while the volume and name of reporters differ, the page number is the same. If the pagination is not identical, use the standard parallel citation form.

EXAMPLE: Wadsworth v. Ruggles, 23 Mass. 62, 6 Pick. 63.

The list of reporters in the back of the Bluebook gives the years for which parallel citations are necessary.

3. Spacing

The general rule is to close up adjacent single capital letters and to separate capital letters when they begin longer abbreviations. For purposes of this rule, a single-digit numeral is treated as a single capital.

EXAMPLES: B.T.A. (close up)
F.2d (close up)
F. Supp. (space between; "Supp." is not a single capital letter)
Ct. Cl. (space between)
L. Ed. 2d (space between)

4. Periods

When the name of the reporter consists of a series of initials, *retain* the periods.

EXAMPLE: N.L.R.B.

5. Parallel Citations

If the state-by-state list in the Bluebook shows that the court or agency had both an official and an unofficial source as of the date of the opinion, include both. If you are citing to a very recent case, the official citation may not yet be available. Cite instead to the "preferred unofficial" source.

EXAMPLE: Wilson v. Lewis, 165 Cal. Rptr. 396.

EXERCISE 5

In the following examples, assume that the name of the case is cited correctly. Check the citation to make sure that the reporter has been cited properly, that the spacing is correct, and that the page number given is the one on which the opinion begins.

1. Eastern Air Lines v. United States, 132 F.S. 787.
2. Early v. Heath, 170 F2d 70, aff'g 77 F. Supp. 474.
3. Garlinger v. Garlinger, 137 N. J. Super., 347 At. 2d 801.
4. In re Marriage of Lusk, 86 Cal. App. 3rd, 228, 150 Cal. Rptr. 63.
5. Frank Lyon Co. v. United States, 435 U.S. 584 (Stevens, J., dissenting).

EXERCISE 6

The following citations may not contain the correct volume and page number, may not be to the official reporter, or may not list all components of the parallel citation. Using the helpful tips given in the preceding chapter, locate the correct citation and put it in the proper form. Do not add the name of the court or date.

1. Go Getter Tug, 398 F.2d 837.
2. Eastern Motor Export v. United States, 344 U.S. 298, 97 L. Ed 337.
3. Greenberg v. Union National Bank, 67 N.W. 1st 597 (5 N.D. 483).
4. People v. Miller, 39 A. D. 2d 893, 343 N.Y.S.2d 252.
5. State v. Crudup, 176 N. J. Super. A. D. 215, _____ A.2d _____.

E. COURT AND JURISDICTION

Every case citation must indicate in a parenthetical following the page number or numbers the name of the court in which the case was decided.

EXAMPLE: Lauterbach v. United States, 95 F. Supp. 479 (W.D. Wash.).

1. Federal Court Cases

At the federal level, each state has one or more district courts, designated geographically (e.g., middle district of Tennessee [M.D. Tenn.], southern district of Florida [S.D. Fla.], or district of Connecticut [D. Conn.]). The states are grouped into numbered circuits for purposes of appealing decisions of the trial courts. These circuits are illustrated on a map in front of every reporter in the West reporter system. There are eleven numbered circuits, plus the D.C. Circuit and Federal Circuit. U.S. circuit court opinions may be appealed to the Supreme Court.

All district court designations are abbreviated by initial capital letters (N.D., E.D., and so on). The name of the state in which the court is located is abbreviated according to the table listed on the inside back cover of the Bluebook. If there is only one district court serving the state, simply abbreviate to "D." followed by the state abbreviation. Do not give the subdivision, such as "E.D. Tenn., W. Div."

Circuit courts are abbreviated as shown on the following list:

1st Cir.	4th Cir.	7th Cir.	10th Cir.	Fed. Cir.
2d Cir.	5th Cir.	8th Cir.	11th Cir.	
3d Cir.	6th Cir.	9th Cir.	D.C. Cir.	

At the Supreme Court level, it is not necessary to indicate the name of the court in parentheses, because the name of the reporter conveys that fact. When citing to U.S. Law Week, it is necessary to *include* "U.S." in the parenthetical, because the general edition publishes reports of other jurisdictions.

Citations contained in early drafts of briefs will sometimes not contain all the information needed for a complete citation. It will then be necessary to obtain the remaining information from the reported case itself.

EXERCISE ⬚7

Obtain the correct information for the following cites from the reporter and put them into the proper form. Do not worry about the date.

1. Lewis v. Pennington, 257 F. Supp. 815 (D.C. Tenn.), aff'd in part and rev'd in part, 400 F.2d 806 (D.C. Tenn.), cert. denied, 393 U.S. 983 (S. Ct.).
2. Parker v. Anderson-Prichard Oil Corp., 245 F.2d 831 (C.A.N.M.).
3. Crown Aluminum Industries Corp. v. NLRB, 327 F.2d 351 (CA 3).
4. In re Crown Cartridge Corp., 220 F. Supp. 914 (D.C.N.Y.).
5. Eli Lilly & Co. v. Brenner, 375 F.2d 599 (U.S. App. D.C. 171).

2. State Court Cases

Each state has its own hierarchy of courts. These are listed in the back of the Bluebook, beginning on page 136. For each state listed, the highest court is shown first. Your first step is to examine the list of courts and their reporters and instructions for parallel citations if required.

Once the first part of the citation has been completed, your next step is to determine what information can then be eliminated from the parenthetical.

(a) If the decision is made by the highest state court, it is not necessary to identify the court in the citation. It will be understood that the decision is of the highest court.

EXAMPLE: Goddard v. General Motors Corp., 60 Ohio St. 2d 41, 396 N.E.2d 761.

(1) In this example, the highest court in Ohio is the Ohio Supreme Court. The Bluebook indicates that Supreme Court cases from 1852 to date are contained in Ohio State Reports, cited as "Ohio St." or "Ohio St. 2d." It also indicates that a parallel citation to N.E. or N.E.2d is needed.

(2) Because the decision is of the highest court of the state, there is no need to give the court in the parenthetical. Because the name of the reporter reveals that the jurisdiction is Ohio, that information can be deleted as well.

(3) *Result:* The parenthetical has no information about either the court or the jurisdiction.

(b) The following example is of an Illinois court decision at the intermediate court level: Palmer v. Liquor Control Commission.

(1) The Bluebook says to "Cite to Ill. App., Ill. App. 2d, or Ill. App. 3d and to N.E.2d."

EXAMPLE: Palmer v. Liquor Control Comm'n, 77 Ill. App. 3d 725, 396 N.E.2d 325.

(2) Because the decision was of an intermediate court, it will be necessary to indicate the court in parentheses. The Bluebook indicates that the proper citation is Palmer v. Liquor Control Commission, 77 Ill. App. 3d 725, 396, N.E.2d 325 (App. Ct.).

(3) Because the name of the reporter discloses that the jurisdiction is Illinois, there is no need to repeat "Ill." in the parenthetical.

(c) The final example is of a case in Florida, a jurisdiction that has abolished official reporters, and so there is no parallel citation.

EXAMPLE: Groff v. Moses, 344 So. 2d 951.

(1) The court is the district court of appeal (not the highest court). Your parenthetical will include: (Dist. Ct. App.).

(2) Because there is no indication from the rest of the citation that the jurisdiction is Florida, that information must be added to the parenthetical. In state cases, the name of the state is given first: (Fla. Dist. Ct. App.).

EXERCISE 8

The following citations contain all the information needed to complete the cite. Your job is to eliminate any unnecessary information from the parenthetical, use the proper abbreviations, and make sure everything is in the correct order. For purposes of this exercise, omit the date.

1. G & S Land, Transportation & Development Corp. v. Yarbrough, 153 Ga. App. 644, 266 S.E.2d 508 (Ga. Ct. App.).

2. Bouvia v. Atlantic Testing Laboratory, 50 A.D.2d 680, 375 N.Y.S.2d 204 (Sup. Ct., App. Div., 3rd Dept. N.Y.).

3. People v. Dalton, 24 Cal. 3d 850, 157 Cal. Rptr. 497, 598 P.2d 467 (Sup. Ct. Cal.).

4. Morton v. United States, 415 A.2d 800 (Ct. App. D.C.).

5. Alexander & Alexander, Inc. v. Central Penn Nat'l Bank, ____ Pa. Super. Ct. ____, 421 A.2d 220 (Super. Ct. Pa.).

3. Agency Actions

The rules for agency decisions are similar to those for state courts (only simpler). If the decision is cited in an *official agency reporter* or in a service that prints only decisions of a single agency, the name of the agency need not be given in the parenthetical. If a loose-leaf service that publishes decisions of courts as well as agencies is the source, then *include* the name of the agency in the parenthetical, even if the name of the service suggests the name of the agency.

EXAMPLE: John H. Wood Co. v. Commissioner, 46 B.T.A. 895 (1969).

(Because the reporter is an official agency reporter, the name of the agency is not included in the parenthetical.)

EXAMPLE: Adams Express Co., [1974–1975 Transfer Binder] Fed. Sec. L. Rep. (CCH) ¶ 80,043 (S.E.C. 1974).

(Because the loose-leaf service publishes decisions of courts as well as those of the S.E.C., the name of the agency must be included in the parenthetical.)

A list of official agency reporters appears on pages 135–36 of the Bluebook.

*4. Advisory Opinions

Formal advisory opinions issued by the attorney general or similar office of a governmental agency are cited in a manner similar to cases.

EXAMPLE: 21 Op. Att'y Gen. 167 (1895).

The name of the opinion may be included as well.

EXAMPLE: Status of the Pacific Northwest River Basin Commission Under the Federal Unemployment Tax Act, 2 Op. Off. Legal Counsel 177 (1978).

If a recent opinion appears only in separately paginated (or un-numbered) advance sheets, omit the page number and indicate the volume and issue number of the advance sheet, as well as the full date.

EXAMPLE: 43 Op. Att'y Gen. No. 1 (Sept. 6, 1974).

F. DATES

**1. Exact Date of Decision

Give the full date of decision for all unreported cases and for cases cited to newspapers, periodicals, and loose-leaf services, regardless of how old the decision is. Use the abbreviations for months given in the inside back cover of the Bluebook.

EXAMPLE: Allstate Ins. Co. v. Hague, 49 U.S.L.W. 4071 (U.S. Jan. 13, 1981).

**2. Year of Decision

In all other cases (including cases appearing in hardbound unof-ficial reporters), only the year of decision is given. Do not confuse the date the case is argued with the date of its decision. (Often, both dates appear in the opinion.) There should be a space between the page number and the parenthetical containing the date.

EXAMPLE: <u>Wunsch v. Wunsch</u>, 248 Wis. 29 (1945).

*3. Date Unknown

If the year of decision is unknown, use the year of the term of court. (Dates of Supreme Court cases, which are usually not given in official reports prior to 108 U.S., may be found in the Lawyer's Edition, beginning with the December 1854 term).

4. Pending Cases

If a case is pending (that is, a final decision has not yet been made), use the date or year of the most recent major disposition (for example, filing of the complaint or granting of certiorari). Indicate the event corresponding to the date either in the prior history of the case or within the parenthetical.

EXAMPLE: <u>Gulf Offshore Co. v. Mobil Oil Corp.</u>, 594 S.W.2d 496 (Tex. 1979), <u>cert. granted</u>, 49 U.S.L.W. 3428 (U.S. Dec. 8, 1980) (No. 80-590).

Note that in *pending* Supreme Court Cases, the Supreme Court docket number is given in parentheses after the date. Other examples appear on page 49 of the Bluebook.

5. Two or More Decisions in the Same Year

In citing a case having two or more decisions in the same year, give the date in the most recent decision only. Eliminate the date in the earlier decision.

EXAMPLE: <u>Chromalloy American Corp. v. Sun Chemical Corp.</u>, 474 F. Supp. 1341 (E.D. Mo.), <u>aff'd</u>, 611 F.2d 240 (8th Cir. 1979).

However, if the exact date of decision is required in either decision, include both dates even if both took place the same year. This format will save confusion.

EXAMPLE: <u>Weingarten v. Block</u>, 102 Cal. App. 3d 129, 162 Cal. Rptr. 701 (1980), <u>cert. denied</u>, 49 U.S.L.W. 3270 (U.S. Oct. 14, 1980).

6. Date in Citation

When citing to a report that uses a date at the beginning of the citation instead of a volume number, it is not necessary to include the date in parentheses at the end, unless the two dates differ.

EXAMPLE: United States v. Safeway Stores, Inc., 1970 Trade Cas. (CCH) ¶ 73,257 (N.D. Tex.).

EXERCISE ⑨

Complete the following citations with parentheticals containing the name of the jurisdiction and date and put them into the correct form. Assume that the given citation is the most recent available source.

1. Blake v. City of Los Angeles, 595 F.2d 1367, cert. denied, 100 S. Ct. 1865.

2. Fullilove v. Beame, 48 N.Y.2d 376, 398 N.E.2d 765, 423 N.Y.S.2d 144.

3. Stevens v. Airline Pilots Association International, 413 A.2d 1305, cert. denied, 49 U.S.L.W. 3511.

4. United States v. Mar-Tee Contractors, Inc., Envtl. L. Rep. (Envtl. L. Inst.) 20,417.

5. State v. Matsen, 26 Crim. L. Rep. (BNA) 2313.

4 | *How to Cite Legislative History Materials and Rules and Regulations*

This chapter briefly describes bills, resolutions, hearings, congressional reports, documents, committee prints and debates, and the proper form for citing these materials. It also discusses published and unpublished sources of legislative histories and illustrates parallel citation forms to these sources. Finally, the proper forms for citing quasi-statutory materials (such as ordinances, regulations, presidential materials, rules of evidence or procedure, and court rules) are included.

A. LEGISLATIVE HISTORY MATERIALS

It is often useful, when urging an interpretation of a particular statutory provision, to discuss the intent of the statute as revealed in the materials generated by the legislative process. These materials can be briefly described as follows.

1. Bills

Each legislative proposal begins as a printed bill, companion versions of which may be introduced in the House and the Senate. They are cited by reference to the bill number, Congress, session, section number (if applicable), and date.

EXAMPLE: H.R. 1491, 97th Cong., 1st Sess. (1981).
EXAMPLE: S. 327, 97th Cong., § 203, 1st Sess. (1981).

A bill that has been introduced but not enacted into law should be cited as shown in these examples but, in addition, should include a citation to either the <u>Congressional Record</u> or to a published hearing that includes a copy of the bill.

EXAMPLE: S. 329, 97th Cong., 1st Sess., 127 Cong. Rec. S781 (daily ed. Jan. 29, 1981).

EXAMPLE: H.R. 12,429, 95th Cong., 2d Sess., <u>Deduction for Self-Insurance for Product Liability: Hearings on H.R. 7711, H.R. 8064, H.R. 10,272, and H.R. 12,429 Before the Subcomm. on Miscellaneous Revenue Measures of the House Comm. on Ways and Means</u> 13 (1978).

NOTE: See Sections 3 and 7 of this chapter for further instructions on how to cite to the <u>Congressional Record</u> and published hearings.

2. Resolutions

Either the House or the Senate may also introduce resolutions. Resolutions may be designated as simple, joint, or concurrent. Joint resolutions are similar in character to bills and, if adopted, are enacted into law in the same manner as bills. Simple and concurrent resolutions are more limited in purpose and are generally used for expressing opinions and the like. Simple resolutions are introduced for matters concerning either the House or the Senate alone; concurrent resolutions are used for matters affecting both sides.

The following abbreviations are used in citing resolutions, no matter what abbreviation appears on the document itself: H.R. Res., S. Res., H.R. Con. Res., S. Con. Res., H.R.J. Res., S.J. Res.

Citations to resolutions include the same basic information as bills (that is, number, Congress, session, and date). In addition, a published source must be indicated, as shown in the following.

(a) Simple Resolutions. Cite simple resolutions to the <u>Congressional Record</u>.

EXAMPLE: H.R. Res. 50, 97th Cong., 1st Sess., 127 Cong. Rec. H276 (daily ed. Jan. 29, 1981).

(b) Joint or Concurrent Resolutions. Cite joint or concurrent resolutions to <u>Statutes at Large</u>.

EXAMPLE: H.R. Con. Res. 664, 94th Cong., 2d Sess., 90 Stat. 3066 (1976).

* If a joint resolution has not yet appeared in <u>Statutes at Large</u>, cite to either a loose-leaf service, a periodical, or a newspaper as follows:

EXAMPLE: S.J. Res. 85, 96th Cong., 1st Sess., [1979–1980] 1 Cong. Index (CCH) 16,505 (1979).

* If a concurrent resolution has not yet appeared in <u>Statutes at Large</u>, cite to the <u>Congressional Record</u>, as follows:

EXAMPLE: S. Con. Res. 111, 95th Cong., 2d Sess., 124 Cong. Rec. S18,145 (daily ed. Oct. 11, 1978).

** Note that numbers containing *five or more digits* are separated by commas.

3. Hearings

After a bill has been introduced, hearings may be held by one or both houses of Congress. Hearings on significant bills may last several months and may include testimony of numerous witnesses.

When citing to a hearing, always include the title of the hearing, the bill number, the name of the committee or subcommittee, the Congress and session, the page number, and the date. If you wish, you may refer to the name of the witness parenthetically. (Note the distinction between prepared statements and live testimony.) It may be necessary to rearrange the information appearing on the cover of the hearing transcript to conform to the format shown in the following example.

EXAMPLE: <u>Customs Procedural Reform Act of 1977: Hearings on H.R. 8149 and H.R. 8222 Before the Subcomm. on Trade of the House Comm. on Ways and Means</u>, 95th Cong., 1st Sess. 628 (1977) (statement of Richard H. Miller).

4. Reports

Following the hearings, the sponsoring committees will amend the bills and prepare a report (called Senate report or House report). After debates and further amendments are made, a conference report (designated as either a House or a Senate report) is prepared by a committee consisting of members of both the House and Senate. These reports are to be abbreviated as follows: H.R. Rep., S. Rep.

As in other legislative materials, include in the citation the report number, Congress and session, page number, and date. In citing the report number, delete the first two digits, which indicate the numbered session of Congress.

EXAMPLE: H.R. Rep. No. 912, 92d Cong., 2d Sess. 20 (1972).

(In this example, the report itself is numbered "92–912." The "92–" is deleted in the citation.)

The legislative history of major legislation is reprinted in the United States Code Congressional and Administrative News. Citations to congressional reports should include a parallel citation to this source as well.

EXAMPLE: S. Rep. No. 416, 96th Cong., 2d Sess. 13 (1979), reprinted in 1980 U.S. Code Cong. & Ad. News 1936, 1943.

**Brackets are no longer used to enclose the date of publication for United States Code Congressional and Administrative News.

5. Federal Documents

From time to time, Congress may publish or authorize studies on areas of proposed legislation and the like. Some of these materials are published as numbered federal documents. These documents are cited in a manner similar to reports.

EXAMPLE: S. Doc. No. 144, 94th Cong., 1st Sess. 138 (1975).

When citing to federal documents, use the following abbreviations: H.R. Doc., S. Doc., H.R. Exec. Doc., H.R. Misc. Doc.

The title of the document may also be given. If so, the name of the institutional author must be cited too, as follows:

EXAMPLE: American School for the Deaf, Report of the Proceedings
of the Forty-Third Meeting of the Convention of American Instructors of the Deaf, S. Doc. No. 59, 90th Cong.,
1st Sess. (1967).

6. Committee Prints

If the study is published by a particular congressional committee, it
is designated as a committee print on the cover and will not be given a
document number. Citations to such works should include the name
of the institutional author, followed by the Congress, session, and title
of the work. The designation "Committee Print" is included in the
parentheses.

EXAMPLE: House Select Comm. on Aging, 94th Cong., 1st Sess.,
Federal Responsibility to the Elderly 12–13 (Comm.
Print 1975).

7. Debates

Once a bill has been reported out of committee, it is introduced
on the floor and open to debate. Such debates are published in the
Congressional Record.

The Congressional Record is published each day that Congress is
in session. Eventually, the daily editions are published in a permanently bound edition employing a different page numbering system. When citing to a congressional debate, cite to the permanent
edition, if available, and otherwise to the daily edition.

EXAMPLE: Permanent edition: 123 Cong. Rec. 33,643 (1977).
Daily edition: 127 Cong. Rec. H263 (daily ed. Jan. 29,
1981).

Note that for the daily edition the date is given in full.

*Debates prior to 1873 are cited to the Annals of Congress, to the
Congressional Debates, or to the Congressional Globe, using the
forms illustrated on page 75 of the Bluebook.

*8. Legislative Histories

In addition to the legislative histories reprinted in the United
States Code Congressional and Administrative News, some com-

pilations are published by congressional, agency, or commercial sources. If any congressional materials described previously appear in such a history, you may include a parallel citation, as follows:

EXAMPLE: House Debate on H.R. 9757, 100 Cong. Rec. 11,020–90 (1954), reprinted in 3 Atomic Energy Comm'n, Legislative History of the Atomic Energy Act of 1954, at 2872– 942 (1955).

Additional sources of legislative history are those assembled by private law firms or trade associations. These are often available on loan. A parallel citation would not be appropriate with such materials unless the pages within the history are consecutively numbered.

EXERCISE ☐1

The following materials are all part of the legislative history of the Atomic Energy Act of 1954. Put the citations into correct form.
1. Sen. Bill 3323, 83rd Congress, 2nd Sess., April 19, 1954.
2. H.J. Res. 555, 83d Cong., 2d Sess., July 2, 1954.
3. Conf. Rep., House Report No. 2639 on H.R. 9757 (83rd Cong., 2d Sess. 1954).
4. S3323 and HR8862 to Amend the Atomic Energy Act of 1946, Hearings Before the Joint Committee on Atomic Energy, 83d Cong., 2d. Sess., May 12, 1954, p. 25 (statement of Jerome D. Luntz).
5. 100 Cong. Rec. 4933 (perm. ed. Apr. 15, 1954).

B. QUASI-STATUTORY MATERIALS

The remainder of this chapter will describe several types of rules, regulations, and orders issued by bodies other than legislatures.

1. Ordinances
An ordinance is an enactment of a city, county, or other local subdivision. The citation should include the name of the locality, the state, the name of the code (if applicable), the section number, and the year of publication.

EXAMPLE: Arlington County, Va., Zoning Ordinance § 12 (1950).

*Uncodified ordinances are cited by number and full date of adoption. Unnumbered ordinances are cited by name.

EXAMPLE: Washington, D.C. Ordinance No. 66–313 (Mar. 8, 1966).

2. Regulations
In addition to their authority to issue opinions, federal administrative agencies have authority to issue regulations, within the limits prescribed by their enabling legislation.

(a) Federal Register. Agency regulations first appear in proposed form in the Federal Register (published daily). When made final, the regulation will likewise first appear in the Federal Register. In addition, the Federal Register publishes various types of agency announcements such as notices of hearings, meetings, or proposed rule making. These are cited as follows:

**EXAMPLE: Meeting Notice, 45 Fed. Reg. 82,125 (1980).
**EXAMPLE: 46 Fed. Reg. 920 (1981) (to be codified at 12 C.F.R. pt. 701) (proposed Jan. 5, 1981).

(b) Code of Federal Regulations. Eventually, final agency rules will be incorporated into the multivolumed Code of Federal Regulations, to be cited as follows:

EXAMPLE: 22 C.F.R. § 16.1 (1979).

The date is the year shown on the spine.
If the C.F.R. citation can be ascertained from the Federal Register notice, indicate both as follows:

EXAMPLE: 45 Fed. Reg. 84,993 (1980) (to be codified at 19 C.F.R. pt. 162).

In citing to federal rules, the name of the regulation may be included in the citation.

EXAMPLE: Fair Housing Advertising Guidelines, 24 C.F.R. pt. 109 (1979).

(c) Treasury Regulations.

(1) Regulations of the Treasury Department are not cited to C.F.R., but use the following form:

EXAMPLE: Treas. Reg. § 342.5 (1971).

The date is the year of adoption, as set forth in a footnote below the text of the regulation as it appears in C.F.R.

(2) If the regulation has been amended or for any other reason has appeared in different versions, expand the citation to include a source that contains the changed language.

EXAMPLE: Treas. Reg. 108, § 86.16a, T.D 5902, 1952–1 C.B. 167.

In this example, the changed language was contained in Treasury Decision 5902, published in Cumulative Bulletin. The date of decision (1952) need not be repeated.

3. Presidential Materials

Presidential materials include executive orders, proclamations, reorganization plans, papers, speeches, and documents. These appear in numerous sources but are to be cited as follows:

(a) Executive Orders. If possible, cite by page number to 3 C.F.R. (which contains presidential issuances for the year of publication), and include a parallel citation to the United States Code or to United States Code Annotated, if not yet published in the official code.

EXAMPLE: Exec. Order No. 12,111, 3 C.F.R. 353 (1979), reprinted in
5 U.S.C. § 5317 n. (Supp. IV 1980).

Generally, such materials are set forth in either a footnote or an appendix to a statute.

If the material is not yet in C.F.R., cite to the Federal Register.

EXAMPLE: Exec. Order 12,174, 44 Fed. Reg. 69,609 (1979).

*(b) Presidential Proclamations and Reorganization Plans.
These materials are cited similarly to executive orders.

EXAMPLE: Pres. Proc. 4697, 3 C.F.R. 77 (1979), <u>reprinted in</u> 19 U.S.C. § 1202 (Supp. IV 1980).

EXAMPLE: Reorg. Plan. No. 2 of 1979, 3 C.F.R. 510 (1979), <u>reprinted in</u> 5 U.S.C. app. II, at 367 (Supp. IV 1980).

A parallel citation to <u>Statutes at Large</u> may also be given.

EXAMPLE: Reorg. Plan No. 2 of 1979, 3 C.F.R. 510 (1979), <u>reprinted in</u> 5 U.S.C. app. II, at 367 (Supp. IV 1980) <u>and in</u> 93 Stat. _____ (1979).

To locate the parallel citations, consult the tables appearing in U.S.C. or U.S.C.A.

*(c) *Papers, Speeches, and Documents.* The preferred source is the <u>Public Papers of the Presidents</u> series, published from 1945 to date.

EXAMPLE: Remarks of Lyndon B. Johnson at the East-West Center in Honolulu, 2 Pub. Papers 1219 (1966).

For material not appearing in <u>Public Papers</u>, cite to <u>The Weekly Compilation of Presidential Documents</u> or to the <u>United States Code Congressional and Administrative News</u>.

EXAMPLE: Letter of Jimmy Carter to Sen. Richard Stone on Panama Canal Treaties, 14 Weekly Comp. Pres. Doc. 227 (Jan. 27, 1978).

EXAMPLE: Inaugural Address of Harry S. Truman, 1949 U.S. Code Cong. & Ad. News 2479.

4. Rules of Evidence or Procedure, Court Rules

Rules of court procedure or practice are cited as follows. If the rule is currently in force, it is not necessary to give the date.

EXAMPLE: Fed. R. Evid. 601.

EXAMPLE: Fed. R. Civ. P. 23(a).

When citing to a court rule, use the court abbreviations given in the Bluebook.

EXAMPLE: D.C. Super. Ct. R. Crim. P. 40-I.

*Rules no longer in force are cited to the latest official source in which they appear, and the date of adoption is included in the citation.

EXAMPLE: Sup. Ct. R. 5, 346 U.S. 953 (1954).

EXERCISE ②

Put the following citations into the proper form.

1. Arlington County, Virginia Zoning Ordinance, Sec. 19, as contained in the Appendix of the Arlington County Code (eff. August 10, 1950 and amendments through Dec. 31, 1980).
2. E.O. 12235, 45, F.R. 58803 (1980).
3. 45 F.R. 58837, to be codified, 21 CFR Part 182, 1980.
4. Treasury Reg. No. 346.2, 31 C.F.R. (promulgated at 40 Fed. Reg. 4240, Jan. 28, 1975).
5. Executive Order No. 11805, 39 Fed. Reg. 34261 (1974), 26 U.S.C. § 6103n. (1976).
6. Interview with the President, Jan. 29, 1980, Weekly Compilation of Presidential Documents, Vol. 16, No. 5, p. 239.
7. Federal Rule of Appellate Procedure, Rule 45(a).
8. 8 CFR § 245.4 (1980).
9. Va. Supreme Court Rule 3A:21 (1977).

5 | *How to Cite Constitutions and Statutory Materials*

This chapter shows the proper form for citing federal and state constitutions and statutes and distinguishes between codified and uncodified enactments. It describes how to update a statutory citation, including the use of <u>Shepard's Citations to Statutes</u>, and gives examples of special short forms for citing certain types of legislation.

A. CONSTITUTIONS

Constitutions are generally published along with the laws of a jurisdiction in a separate volume. The United States Constitution appears as part of the <u>United States Code Annotated</u> (published by West).

1. Constitutions are cited by country or state and the abbreviation "Const.," followed by reference to article, and if applicable, section and clause, as follows:

EXAMPLE: U.S. Const. art. I, § 8, cl. 4.

Amendments to the Constitution are cited as follows:

EXAMPLE: U.S. Const. amend. XIII, § 1.

*2. Ordinarily, the date is not given. There are two instances when the date is given, however. The first is when a particular provision has been repealed or amended and thus is no longer in effect as cited. Such provisions are cited as follows:

EXAMPLE: Cal. Const. art. XII, § 24 (1879, repealed 1972).

*3. If a particular constitution has been totally superseded, cite the year of adoption as part of the title.

EXAMPLE: Ark. Const. of 1836, art. VII, § 2.

*4. If a specific provision in an outdated constitution was adopted in a different year from that in which the constitution was adopted, indicate both dates as follows:

EXAMPLE: Ark. Const. of 1836, amend. 4 (1846).

B. FEDERAL STATUTES

A brief understanding of the legislative process will enhance your grasp of how to cite to statutory materials. Following is a brief description of the statutory sources you will encounter.

1. Once a bill is passed by both houses and enacted into law, it receives a consecutive public law number. (From the 85th Congress on, the first two digits of the public law number correspond to the numbered Congress currently in session.) It is first published in pamphlet form as a slip law.

EXAMPLE: Pub. L. No. 96–153.

2. Many acts are also known by either a formal or a popular name, designated in the act itself. If no name appears in the act itself, it may be referred to by its date of enactment. These names form the first part of a statutory citation.

EXAMPLE: Federal Interstate Land Sales Full Disclosure Act.
EXAMPLE: Act of June 26, 1948.

3. Each new law is also published in a multivolume compilation, Statutes at Large, a chronological arrangement of laws as they are enacted.

EXAMPLE: 93 Stat. 1101.

The public law number, together with its citation to Statutes at Large, form the reference to "session laws" (that is, as first enacted).

4. Eventually, the act will be codified; that is, its sections will be renumbered and arranged in one of the existing fifty titles of the United States Code. (Each title corresponds to a separate subject matter.) If the new law amends, repeals, or supplements certain provisions of an existing law, the codification will reflect the entire law as amended.

EXAMPLE: 15 U.S.C. §§ 1701–1720.

Thus, a given statutory provision will ultimately have two section numbers: one as originally enacted and the other as codified. For example, Pub. L. No. 96–153, § 401 corresponds to 15 U.S.C. § 1701.

5. The United States Code (U.S.C.), the official compilation, is published every six years with the year of publication indicated on the spine. At the conclusion of each session of Congress, the main volume is updated by numbered hardbound supplement volumes. These supplements are cumulative—that is, each new supplement updates and replaces the previous ones. After the fifth supplement is published, an updated Code is prepared and the process is repeated.

**6. Unofficial federal codes include the United States Code Annotated (U.S.C.A.), published by West, and the United States Code Service (U.S.C.S.), published by the Lawyers Co-operative Publishing Company (abbreviated "Law. Co-op."). Each compilation contains, in addition to the text of statutes, historical footnotes and annotations to law review articles and cases construing various statutory provisions. They are updated annually by means of a pocket part and further updated by means of paperbound advance sheets. These must all be consulted to obtain a complete citation.

7. New laws may also be reprinted in a loose-leaf service, a periodical, or a newspaper.

Following is an explanation of the rules for citing statutes.

(a) When giving a statutory citation, you should cite to either the United States Code, an unofficial code, the session laws, or a secondary source—in that order of preference.

(1) United States Code.

EXAMPLE: Interstate Land Sales Full Disclosure Act of 1979, 15
U.S.C. §§ 1701–1720 (1976 & Supp. IV 1980).

Note that the citation includes the name of the act, the date of the Code appearing on the spine of the main volume, and the date of the supplement. If the act appeared only in the main volume, reference to the supplement would be dropped.

(2) Unofficial code (for enactments too recent to appear in the United States Code).

EXAMPLE: Interstate Land Sales Full Disclosure Act of 1979, § 401,
15 U.S.C.A. § 1701 (West 1982).

Since no date appears on the spine, the year cited is the date given on the title page. (If none is given, then use the date of copyright.) Note that on this and on all statutory citations the original section number of the particular provision cited is included.

(3) Session laws (for statutes not yet codified).

EXAMPLE: Interstate Land Sales Full Disclosure Act of 1979, Pub. L.
No. 96–153, § 401, 93 Stat. 1101, 1122–23.

In this example, the date of enactment (1979) appears as part of the name of the act. If the date of enactment is not reflected in the name of the act, or is different from that shown, include the date parenthetically after the page number of the session laws.

EXAMPLE: National Environmental Policy Act of 1969, Pub. L. No.
91–190, 83 Stat. 852 (1970).

(4) Secondary source (for statutes too recent to appear in either the Code or session laws).

EXAMPLE: Interstate Land Sales Full Disclosure Act of 1979, Pub. L.
No. 96–153, § 401, 1 Land Dev. L. Rep. (Land Dev.
Inst.) 1-A1 to 1-A2 (1980) (to be codified at 15 U.S.C.
§ 1701).

**The preferred secondary source is United States Code Congressional and Administrative News. Include parenthetically in the citation the volume number of Statutes at Large; the page number will be the same for both sources. This and all other information to be included in the citation is contained on the first page of the statute, as reprinted.

EXAMPLE: Interstate Land Sales Full Disclosure Act of 1979, Pub. L.
No. 96–153, § 401, 1979 U.S. Code Cong. & Ad. News
(93 Stat.) 1101, 1122–23.

When citing to the act as a whole, the section number would be omitted, as well as the pinpoint cite to Statutes at Large. Information regarding its codification, if known, is given parenthetically.

(b) When referring to the enactment of a statute (or its amendment or repeal) for its historical significance, cite to the session laws and indicate its codification parenthetically. You may, if you wish, for the sake of clarity, include the effective date in parentheses.

EXAMPLE: The Interstate Land Sales Full Disclosure Act was originally enacted in 1968. Pub L. No. 90–448, 82 Stat. 476
(1968) (effective Apr. 28, 1969).

*(c) If a particular statute is no longer in force as cited, the citation *must* indicate that fact. In the following example, the cited statute has subsequently been amended and renumbered.

EXAMPLE: Act of Mar. 3, 1883, ch. 123, § 2, 22 Stat. 527 (1939) (current version at 39 U.S.C. § 2005 (1976)).

EXAMPLE: 39 U.S.C. § 739 (repealed 1960).

(d) When citing to the current version of a statute, prior history *may* be given parenthetically, if relevant to the discussion.

EXAMPLE: 39 U.S.C. § 2005 (1976) (originally enacted as Act of Mar. 3, 1883, ch. 123, § 2, 22 Stat. 527).

(e) When citing to a statute or its amendment, cite to the current Code or its supplement or both, depending on which volumes contain the language used.

EXAMPLES: Current code: Civil Obedience Act of 1968, 18 U.S.C. § 231 (1976).
Supplement: Earthquake Hazards Reduction Act of 1977, 42 U.S.C. §§ 7701–7706 (Supp. IV 1980).
Both: Interstate Land Sales Full Disclosure Act of 1979, 15 U.S.C. §§ 1701–1720 (1976 & Supp. IV 1980).

(f) When citing to an unofficial code or its supplement, indicate the name of the publisher in parentheses.

EXAMPLE: Interstate Land Sales Full Disclosure Act of 1979, § 401, 15 U.S.C.A. § 1701 (West 1982).

(g) When a statute as originally enacted is found in the Code and its amendment is available only in an unofficial source, cite as follows:

EXAMPLE: Fish and Wildlife Act of 1956, 16 U.S.C. § 742 (1946), amended by Act of June 28, 1980, Pub. L. No. 96–291 (codified at 16 U.S.C.A. § 742j–2 (West Supp. 1981)).

You may, if you prefer, cite to the most recent enactment and add the prior history parenthetically. Note that if this method is used, the parenthetical information "amending" is *not* italicized; in the prior example, "amended by" is.

EXAMPLE: Pub. L. No. 96–291, 16 U.S.C.A. § 742j–2 (West Supp. 1981) (amending Fish and Wildlife Act of 1956, 16 U.S.C. § 742 (1946)).

(h) When working with statutory citations, do not forget to check the supplements, pocket parts, and advance sheets. You may find that a particular provision thought to be current has been amended or repealed.

*(*i*) When a statute appears in so many scattered sections of the Code that citation to the Code would be awkward, cite instead to the session laws, with references to the Code in parentheses.

EXAMPLE: Federal Trade Commission Improvement Act of 1980, Pub. L. No. 96–252, 94 Stat. 374 (to be codified in scattered sections of 15 U.S.C.).

*(*j*) If a statutory provision is contained in an appendix to a numbered title, cite as follows:

EXAMPLE: Military Selective Service Act, 50 U.S.C.A. app. § 455 (West 1981).

(k) When discussing a particular statute at some length, you may find it useful to give a full citation the first time it is cited, citing to both the session laws and the Code.

EXAMPLE: Interstate Land Sales Full Disclosure Act of 1979, Pub. L. No. 96–153, 93 Stat. 1101 (codified at 15 U.S.C. §§ 1701– 1720 (1976 & Supp. IV 1980)).

Thereafter, citation may be simply to the Code.

EXAMPLE: 15 U.S.C. § 1711.

(l) Following are examples of simplified citation forms to be used for certain types of enactments.

(1) Uniform acts. When not citing to a uniform act as the law of a particular state, cite it as a separate code, giving the year in which the uniform act was last amended, without regard to the particular section cited.

EXAMPLE: Uniform Probate Code § 3–102 (1979).

A citation to <u>Uniform Laws Annotated</u> (a fourteen-volume work published by West) may be given.

EXAMPLE: Uniform Aircraft Financial Responsibility Act, § 8, 12 U.L.A. 24, 37–38 (1954).

Otherwise, cite the uniform act in the same manner as a state statute.

EXAMPLE: Uniform Anatomical Gift Act, Fla. Stat. Ann. §§ 732.910–.921 (West 1981).

(2) Uniform Commercial Code. Cite in abbreviated form, as follows:

EXAMPLE: U.C.C. § 2–201(3) (b) (1977).

**(3) Internal Revenue Code. The current Internal Revenue Code (title 26 of the <u>United States Code</u>) is also cited as a separate codification. The year of the current <u>United States Code</u> or its supplement (whichever is appropriate) should be included in the citation.

EXAMPLE: I.R.C. § 1374 (1976).

In briefs and memoranda intended to be used for a very short time, the date may be omitted.

In all of these examples, if the cited section has been amended or repealed, the date of amendment or repeal would be indicated parenthetically, in a manner similar to citations of outdated constitutional provisions.

(4) Model codes, restatements, standards. Model codes, restatements, and standards, unlike uniform laws, are not adopted by particular states. The citation will include the name of the code, restatement, or standard; the relevant section, rule, or other subdivision; and the date of adoption or the most recent amendment.

EXAMPLE: Model Code of Pre-Arraignment Procedure § SS 240.3 (1975).

If the citation is to the compiler's note, comment, or illustration of the particular material that it follows, include the relevant information in the citation as follows:

EXAMPLE: Restatement (Second) of Contracts § 353 note (1932).

Numbered editions of the restatement are indicated parenthetically in the title, as shown in the previous example.

Tentative or proposed drafts are also designated parenthetically.

EXAMPLE: Restatement of Evidence R. 304 (Tent. Draft No. 1, 1940).

Authors other than the American Bar Association or American Law Institute are also included in the parenthetical.

EXAMPLE: Model Community Noise Control Ordinance § 8.1 (Nat'l Inst. of Mun. Law Officers 1975).

Similar citation forms are used in citing to the ABA Codes of Professional Responsibility and Judicial Conduct, the opinions of the ABA Committee on Ethics and Professional Responsibility (and its predecessors), and the recently proposed Model Rules of Professional Conduct.

EXAMPLE: Model Code of Professional Responsibility DR 4–101 (1979).

EXAMPLE: Model Code of Judicial Conduct Canon 7 (1972).

The formal and informal opinions of the Ethics Committee should include the name of the committee and the number and year of the opinion.

EXAMPLE: ABA Comm. on Professional Ethics, Informal Dec. 799 (1965).

EXERCISE 1

The following citations contain all the information you need for a complete citation. Put each citation into the correct form. If the citation does not use the preferred source, revise it appropriately.

1. 21st Amendment, Section 2, U.S. Constitution.
2. Food Stamp Act Amendments of 1980, § 111, 7 U.S.C.A. § 2012 (1980 West), Pub. L. No. 96–249, 94 Stat. 357, 360–361.
3. Pub. L. No. 96–265, 94 Stat. 453 (June 9, 1980, effective June 1, 1981).
4. 26 U.S.C.A. § 7851 (1976) (Supp. III 1979).
5. Rail Passenger Service Act of 1970, 45 U.S.C.A. § 562, as amended by Passenger Railroad Rebuilding Act of 1980, Pub. L. 96–254, Title II, § 206(a), 94 Stat. 410, 412–13 (amending sections 562, 563, 601, 851, 853, 854), 45 U.S.C.A. § 562 (1980 Supp.) (West).
6. Restatement of the Law of Agency 2nd, § 407, p. 255 (1958).

C. STATE STATUTES

The rules for citing provisions of state codes are analogous to those used in citing to federal statutes. Your first step is to consult the state-by-state listing beginning at page 136 of the Bluebook to obtain the name of the official statutory compilation and session laws to be used. The following additional rules may be relevant. Whenever possible, the official compilation should be used.

Note that some states (such as Virginia) may authorize a particular publisher to issue the official code; in Virginia, for example, the official code is published by the Michie Company. In these states, the table of state materials beginning on page 136 of the Bluebook will omit the name of the publisher in the model citation form.

1. Codified Laws

As indicated on the spine of the volumes, state laws may be set forth in a general code with consecutively numbered volumes, in subject matter codes arranged alphabetically (for example, Domestic Relations, Property, Trusts and Estates), or in a combination of both.

When citing to a state code, give the name of the codification (including the name of the subject matter code, if applicable), the appropriate subdivision, and the year.

The appropriate format for each state will vary. Citation may be to a numbered title, chapter, or volume number. The volume number may precede or follow the codification. You should follow the Bluebook model in citing the code of each state.

EXAMPLES: General code: Kan. Stat. Ann. § 21–3502 (1974).
Subject matter code: Md. Real Prop. Code Ann. § 7–204 (1974).

2. Uncodified Laws

Generally, cite uncodified laws to the session laws.

EXAMPLE: Act of June 10, 1981, No. 129, 1981 Hawaii Sess. Laws 271 (amending Hawaii Rev. Stat. § 88–119 (1976 & Supp. 1981)).

When citing to state session laws, always begin the citation with the name of the statute, or, if none, the date of enactment; the public law or chapter number; the year or volume number of the session laws, followed by the name of the state. The appropriate form for each state is illustrated in the table beginning on page 136 of the Bluebook.

**Occasionally, uncodified statutes may appear in separate volumes (such as McKinney's Unconsolidated Laws of New York, or Deering's Water—Uncodified Acts of California). Rarely, an uncodified statute may appear in an appendix to a particular title of a code.

If the enactment appears in a separate volume, cite to that volume and not the session laws.

EXAMPLE: Contra Costa County Flood Control and Water Conservation District Act, Cal. Water Uncodified Acts act 1656, § 21 (Deering 1970).

If the statute is set forth in an appendix, cite directly to the appendix if the statute is divided into sections as though it were codified.

Otherwise, cite to the session laws, as illustrated previously, followed by reference to its appearance in the appendix. Examples of each type appear on page 62 of the Bluebook, Rule 12.3(g).

3. Sections and Subsections

NOTE: The following rules are applicable to federal as well as state statutes, but are included here because of the greater variety of numbering schemes found among state statutes.

In citing to sections of statutes, follow the punctuation used in the code to separate sections from subsections. If no separating punctuation is given, insert parentheses around the subsection.

EXAMPLE: Ind. Code Ann. § 32-4-1.5-3(a) (West 1979).

When citing to multiple sections or subsections of the code, give inclusive numbers of the sections or subsections to be cited. Do not use et seq.

EXAMPLE: Va. Code §§ 3.1-919 to -969 (1973).

If the section number of a statute is separated by punctuation marks, identical digits *preceding* a punctuation mark may be omitted when citing multiple section numbers.

EXAMPLE: Nev. Rev. Stat. § 497.010-.270 (1979).

In this example, the "497" preceding the second period was omitted.
If a single section number includes hyphens, when citing multiple section numbers, use the word "to" instead of another hyphen to avoid confusion.

EXAMPLE: S.C. Code Ann. §§ 47-15-10 to -80 (Law. Co-op. 1979).

Use only a single section symbol when citing to subsections within the same section.

EXAMPLE: Alaska Stat. § 38.04.020(b)-(d) (1981).

But use *two* section symbols when citing to various subsections within *different* sections.

EXAMPLE: Minn. Stat. Ann. §§ 124.43 (Subd. 1), .46 (Subd. 4) (West 1979).

When in doubt as to whether a particular provision is considered a section or subsection, consult the section index at the beginning of the chapter in the Code.

If the letter *l* is used as a subdivision, it should always be italicized (to avoid confusion with the numeral 1).

EXAMPLE: N.Y. Est., Powers & Trusts Law § 11-2.1(*l*) (McKinney 1967).

*4. Dual Numbering Systems

In a few states (such as Michigan and Pennsylvania), there exist unofficial compilations that employ a numbering system different from that used in the official code. Such sources may be used only if the official citation is not available.

EXAMPLE: 69 Pa. Stat. Ann. §§ 2501–2507 (Purdon Supp. 1979).

In this example, the statute does not yet appear in either the official or preferred unofficial compilations (Pa. Cons. Stat. or Pa. Cons. Stat. Ann.), which, when compiled, will contain a different numbering system.

EXERCISE ☐2

Put the following citations into the proper form, using the table in back of the Bluebook if necessary.

1. Texas Rev. Civ. Stats. Insurance Code, art. 16.25, Vernon, 1963 & 1980 Supp.

2. Illinois 1980 Legis. Service, West, Pub. Act No. 81-1456, approved Sept. 8, 1980.

3. Alabama Worthless Check Act, Title 13, § 13-4-110 (1977) (no amendments in pocket part).

4. Deering's Cal. Code Annot., Business and Professions, § 16200 (1976).

5. Maine Rev. Stat. Ann. § 313 (West Supp. 1978), Vol. 9B.

D. SHEPARD'S CITATIONS TO STATUTES

No discussion of statutory citations would be complete without mentioning the statute edition of Shepard's Citations, available in both federal and state editions.

As in Shepard's Citations to Cases, Shepard's Citations to Statutes shows references to the cited material in opinions by the federal and state courts. In addition, Shepard's indicates the effect of the statutory provision being cited on the operation of the existing statutory framework and shows whether any court has determined its validity. The abbreviations appearing in the margin to the left of the entries indicate such events as whether a statute has been amended ("A"), expanded ("Ad"), repealed ("R"), superseded ("S"), reenacted ("Re-en"), revised ("Rv"), upheld as constitutional ("C"), or found unconstitutional in part ("Up") or in whole ("U"). A full list of abbreviations and their significance appears in the front of each volume of Shepard's.

The format of the entries for statutory provisions is similar to that for cases. The title and year of the code in which the statutory provision appears is given at the top of the page, and the section or sub-section numbers appear in boldface type in numerical order within columns. The entries under each heading list citations to the statute in published opinions, in articles of the American Bar Association Journal, and in annotations, as well as any amendments, repeals, or similar alterations to its status occurring subsequent to 1962. Note that earlier volumes of Shepard's Citations to Statutes will refer to versions of the code no longer in effect. For purposes of cite-checking, it is necessary to consult only the volume of Shepard's corresponding to the code referred to in the citation. For example, if the citation is to the 1976 edition of the United States Code, then you would check only those volumes of Shepard's containing references to the 1976 Code and could disregard the 1968 edition of Shepard's, which referred to the 1964 Code.

The sample entries shown in Illustration 3 give you the following information about the cited statute. (Reference is to title 42 of the <u>United States Code</u>, 1976 edition.)

ILLUSTRATION 3

§ 2135
60ABA921
§ 2139
A92St141
§ 2140
451FS1251
Subsec. a
L88St1244
§ 2141
Ad92St125*

*Reprinted from *Shepard's United States Citations—Statutes, Supplement 1974–1979 to Statute Edition, 1968,* page 543, with permission of the copyright holder. Copyright 1979 by McGraw-Hill, Inc.

1. Section 2135 was cited in an article appearing in the <u>American Bar Association Journal</u>, volume 60, page 921.
2. Section 2139 was amended at 92 Stat. 141.
3. Section 2140 was cited in a U.S. district court case appearing at 451 F. Supp. 1251.
4. The provisions of section 2140(a) were expressly limited in a subsequent amendment of the statute appearing at 88 Stat. 1244.
5. Section 2141 was added by 92 Stat. 125.

Another useful addition to the Shepard's series is <u>Shepard's Acts by Popular Names</u>, which will enable you to obtain the correct citation of federal or state laws, given only the nickname of the act. Unlike the statute edition of <u>Shepard's</u> Citations, all entries, both state and federal, are combined in a single volume, alphabetically by name (for example, "Industrial Mortgage Insurance Act," "Industrial Park Act"). Citations to federal statutes include the public law number as well as its appearance in <u>Statutes at Large</u>. If similar versions of the act appear in a number of state codes, <u>Shepard's</u> will list them all, in alphabetical order by state. Uniform acts, with citations to each state code in which they have been adopted to date, are also listed.

*Another useful source of information on state and federal statutes is The Martindale-Hubbell Law Directory, published annually by Martindale-Hubbell, Inc., and best known for its comprehensive listing of practicing attorneys listed by state and county. Volume VIII of this publication contains digests of laws for each state; the U.S. copyright, patent and trademark laws; the laws of Canada and the Canadian provinces; the laws of other countries; and the uniform and model acts. Volume VIII also reprints the American Bar Association Model Codes of Professional Responsibility and Judicial Conduct. These digests serve as a quick reference tool for a firm that does not have access to the statutes of every state. Once the correct citation is located, the remaining components of the citation can be obtained from the state-by-state listing in the back of the Bluebook. A secondary source such as Martindale-Hubbell's should not be used if the state code is available but should be reserved for situations such as cite-checking a law review article submitted by an out-of-state author, or as an aid in locating the source of an incomplete or inaccurate citation.

EXERCISE 3

In the blanks to the right of the following items, indicate any information that would affect the citation found by using Shepard's United States Citations—Statutes. Consult only those volumes referring to the current edition of the Code. If Shepard's indicates that a different statutory provision from the one cited is now in effect, state where the current provision can be found.

1. 22 U.S.C. § 1439 (1976).   _____

2. 50 U.S.C. § 98b(e) (1976).   _____

3. 10 U.S.C. § 801 (1976).   _____

4. 10 U.S.C. § 717(c) (1976).   _____

5. 7 U.S.C. § 1282a (1976).   _____

6 | *How to Cite Books, Periodicals, Loose-leaf Services, and Other Authorities*

This chapter describes the proper form for citing books, pamphlets, law review articles, periodicals, newspaper articles, materials appearing in loose-leaf services (both bound and unbound), and newsletters. It also shows how to cite to briefs, motions and similar materials filed with a court, as well as unpublished materials such as speeches, letters, interviews, and dissertations. It suggests procedures for cataloging and indexing materials generated in a law firm for quick retrieval.

A. BOOKS AND PAMPHLETS

Citations to books, pamplets, and similar materials must include the following information: author, title, page number (or section or paragraph number), and date of publication. In addition, the following information, if applicable, must be included: volume number; series number; name of editor, publisher, or translator; edition number; and information that may help to locate an unpublished work. The examples that follow will illustrate the rules of citation for each of these components.

1. Volume Number

If a complete work contains two or more volumes, indicate the volume number of the cited work in Arabic numerals as follows:

EXAMPLE: 12 J. Moore, H. Bendix & B. Ringle, <u>Moore's Federal Practice</u> ¶ 506.01, at 8–20 (2d ed. 1980).

2. Author

Authors are ordinarily cited by first initial and last name.

EXAMPLE: W. Ringel, <u>Arrests, Searches, Confessions</u> 112 (1966).

*Additional information (such as the middle initial or such designations as "II" or "Jr.") may be added to avoid confusion in identifying the author, particularly if the surname is a common one or one that may be confused with that of another widely known author.

EXAMPLE: W.O. Douglas, <u>The Bible and the Schools</u> 56 (1966).

If a book has more than one author, list all authors the first time a work is cited. Subsequent references may be by an appropriate "hereinafter" form. Do not use <u>et al.</u>

EXAMPLE: R. Sandison, R. Anderson, I. Faggen, L. Garber, D. Lipson, J. Schwieters & G. Warnick, <u>Federal Taxes Affecting Real Estate</u> 150–51 (4th ed. 1978) [hereinafter cited as Sandison & Anderson].

Note the use of "&" rather than "and" as a connective between coauthors.

Institutional authors are cited by spelling out the name of the author in full. If the author is a subdivision of a larger entity, list the smaller unit first.

EXAMPLE: International Program in Taxation, Harvard Law School, <u>Taxation in the United States</u> ¶ 7/2.12, at 473 (1963).

In citing institutional authors, use only widely recognized abbreviations (such as "Dep't"), and use them sparingly, if at all. When abbreviating, use the forms suggested in the Bluebook for case names in footnotes, as well as the geographical abbreviations listed in the inside back cover. The words "United States" may be abbreviated "U.S."

*When citing to a preface or foreword that is written by someone other than the author of the main work, cite as follows:

EXAMPLE: T. Roosevelt, Introduction to W. Ransom, Majority Rule and the Judiciary 8 (reprint ed. 1971).

Ordinarily, the author of a chapter of a book is cited by last name alone. In the preceding example, the first initial was added for identification purposes.

3. Editor, Publisher, or Translator

Generally, the editor or translator is not included in the citation, *except* in the following situations:

(a) Works that are designated by an editor or publisher rather than an author are cited with the name of the editor or publisher given parenthetically, as follows:

EXAMPLE: 1978 Federal Tax Handbook (Prentice-Hall, Inc. 1978).

(b) In an edited collection of essays by different authors, indicate both the author of the cited essay and the editor (or translator) of the work as a whole. Omit the first initial of the essay author, and underline the title of the essay, as well as the title of the book.

EXAMPLE: Riker, Public Safety as a Public Good, in Is Law Dead? 370 (E. Rostow ed. 1971).

*If a book consists of a collection of essays by the same author, indicate the author as follows:

EXAMPLE: T. Morrisey, Toward a New Environmental Ethic, in Pollution Control Problems and Related Federal Legislation 10 (1975).

4. Title

List the full title that appears on the title page, capitalize the first letter of the first word and the first letter of all other words *except* articles, conjunctions, and prepositions of four letters or less. *Omit the subtitle*, if any, ** unless it is particularly informative. Do not abbreviate words in the title.

EXAMPLE: T. Adams, Law Enforcement 34 (2d ed. 1973).

In this example, the subtitle, "An Introduction to the Police Role in the Criminal Justice System," was not used.

For lengthy titles, you may wish to establish a "hereinafter" form.

EXAMPLE: E. Peffer, Use and Abuse of America's Natural Resources 115 (1972) [hereinafter cited as Resources].

5. Page Number

Indicate the relevant page or page numbers immediately after the title of the work. When citing to multiple page numbers, give the inclusive page numbers, separated by a hyphen. Always *retain* the last two digits, and drop other digits if repetitious.

EXAMPLE: C. Lee, One Man, One Vote 115–17, 189–201 (1967).

* If the title of a book ends with a number, or when the page number is irregular in form (such as a small roman numeral or a hyphenated number), insert the word "at" as follows. Never use "p." in citations to designate a page number.

EXAMPLE: H. Gutman, The Black Family in Slavery and Freedom, 1750–1925, at 180 (1976).
EXAMPLE: 3 J. Moore, Moore's Federal Practice ¶ 13.14[4], at 13–337 to –338 (2d ed. 1980).

6. Series Number

If a publication is one of a series, the series number is included either as part of the *title* or as part of the *parenthetical*, depending on whether the series is issued by the author or someone other than the author. In referring to a series, always include the designation "No." even if the book does not.

EXAMPLES: Series issued by author: Practising Law Institute, Clinical Law and Urban Problems Course Handbook Series No. 22, <u>Legal Control of the Environment</u>—2nd, at 35–40 (1970).
Series issued by other: L. Cohen, <u>Juvenile Dispositions</u> 23 (Utilization of Criminal Justice Statistics Project, Analytic Report No. 4, 1975).

7. Edition

(a) Multiple Editions. A work that appears in only one edition is cited without reference to that fact.

EXAMPLE: S. Searcy, <u>Privacy and Public Records</u> 40–43 (1977).

In works having more than one edition, cite to the latest edition available.

EXAMPLE: C. Wright, <u>Handbook of the Law of Federal Courts</u> 270–72 (2d ed. 1970).

*Cite to an earlier edition or a particular printing only if necessary to support the point under discussion.
*In citing to a particular edition of a work, include such additional information as may be designated on the title page (such as "abridged," "revised,"). A list of abbreviations to be used for that purpose appears on page 84 of the Bluebook.

EXAMPLE: D. Crumbley & P. Davis, <u>Organizing, Operating and Terminating Subchapter S Corporations</u> 151 (rev. ed. 1980).

(b) Star Edition. In a few well-known works that have been reissued with different pagination, the page numbers of the original edition are indicated with an asterisk. In citing to such works, indicate only the page number of the original (star) edition and omit the date and edition from the citation.

EXAMPLE: 1 J. Kent, <u>Commentaries</u> *545.

8. Date

Generally, the date given is the date of the edition and not the date of copyright or printing.

EXAMPLE: A. Casner & R. Stein, Estate Planning Under the Tax Reform Act of 1976, at 73 (2d ed. 1978).

*The date and number of a particular printing would be added to the citation only if the various printings differ in a respect that is relevant for purposes of the citation.

EXAMPLE: (13th ed. 2d printing 1982).

*9. Material Published Prior to 1870

Cite material published prior to 1870 to the *first* edition whenever possible. Include in the parentheses the editor, or, if none, the place of publication.

EXAMPLE: The Lawes Resolutions of Womens Rights; or The Lawes Provision for Women 124–25 (London 1632).

When citing to a later edition (when using material not contained in the earlier edition), give information concerning the first edition parenthetically as follows.

EXAMPLE: J. Elliot, The Debates in the Several State Conventions (2d ed. Wash., D.C. 1836) (1st ed. Wash., D.C. 1830).

If the date or place of publication is not known, indicate this fact by the abbreviation "n.d." or "n.p.," respectively. Cite to an exact reprint of a work as to the original edition, provided the reprint has not altered the original in any significant respect.

EXAMPLE: F. Holt, The Law of Libel 210–15 (1812).

10. Treatises

The following rules, which apply to all books and pamphlets, are particularly applicable to treatises.

**(a) Volume and Author. When citing to a particular volume of a multivolumed treatise, indicate the volume by Arabic numeral and list the authors of the particular volume cited.

EXAMPLE: 12 J. Moore, H. Bendix & B. Ringle, <u>Moore's Federal Practice</u> ¶ 506.01, at 8–20 (2d ed. 1980).

(b) Page Number or Other Subdivision. Treatise entries are often divided into numbered sections or paragraphs. When citing to these subdivisions, use the appropriate symbol "¶" or "§."

EXAMPLE: 8 M. Volz, <u>West's Federal Practice Manual</u> §10,218 (2d ed. 1979).

When citing to a particular page number within a section or paragraph, indicate both designations as follows, if necessary for identification. Do not cite to page numbers alone if a book is divided into sections or paragraphs.

EXAMPLE: 8 C. Wright & A. Miller, <u>Federal Practice and Procedure</u> § 2018, at 143 (1970).

Multiple paragraphs should be treated similarly to multiple sections with respect to separating punctuation.

EXAMPLE: 14A. F. Poore, <u>Cyclopedia of Federal Procedure</u> §§ 73.77–1.82 (rev. 3d ed. 1965).

(c) Supplements. Treatises frequently are updated by means of a pocket part or bound supplement. Cite to the supplement and its date (or, if appropriate, to both the main volume and its supplement) as follows:

EXAMPLE: R. Hunter, <u>Federal Trial Handbook</u> § 42.3 (1974 & Supp. 1980).

If page numbers within the main volume and supplement are included in the citation, use the following form for clear identification:

EXAMPLE: R. Hunter, <u>Federal Trial Handbook</u> § 42.3, at 349 (1974); <u>id</u>. at 119–20 (Supp. 1980).

*11. Location Information

When citing to printed material of limited circulation and to unpublished material, give the exact date, if known, and add information concerning the location of a work parenthetically.

EXAMPLE: R. Schwartz, <u>Welfare Advocate Handbook</u> 11 (2d rev. ed. Apr. 1972)(available from the author, at Welfare Advocate, 1507 Tarbox St., San Diego, Cal. 92114).

12. Special Citation Forms

(a) Encyclopedias. Indicate encyclopedia entries as follows:

EXAMPLE: 43A C.J.S. <u>Injunctions</u> § 222 (1928).

(b) Other Special Citation Forms. Refer to pages 86 and 87 of the Bluebook for examples of how to cite excerpts from the Bible, the <u>Federalist</u> papers, and the <u>Manual for Complex Litigation</u>.

EXERCISE ☐1

Put the following citations into the proper form, eliminating superfluous information. If no change is necessary, indicate "No change."

1. Nat'l Comm'n on the Causes and Prevention of Violence, Firearms and Violence in American Life 111 (1969).   _____

2. C. White III, Writing Effective Proposals, pp. 17–20, ABA Special Committee on Youth Education for Citizenship, The $$ Game, Working Notes No. 7 (1975).   _____

3. A. Avins, ed., Open Occupancy vs. Forced Housing Under the Fourteenth Amendment: A Symposium on Anti-Discrimination Legislation, Freedom of Choice, and Property Rights in Housing. E. Million, Racial Restrictive Covenants Revisited at p. 95 (1963).   _____

4. D. Nedrud and Oberto, M., eds., The Criminal Law A-81 (1971).   _____

5. H. Edwards, V. Nordin, Higher Education and the Law 16 (1980 cum. supp.).   _____

6. James Wigmore, Wigmore on Evidence, vol. 9, § 2461, p. 187 (3rd ed., 1940).   _____

7. H. Burns, Foreword, p. xiv, to <u>White Justice</u> (S. Blackburn ed. 1971).   _____

B. PERIODICALS

1. Identification

A "periodical" is any publication, generally in pamphlet format, published at regular intervals (usually weekly, monthly, or quarterly), containing a variety of articles by various authors. Initially each issue appears separately; later the issues within a single volume may be bound. Usually, the pages within a particular volume of a scholarly periodical are numbered continuously from one issue to the next. Works of more general interest may be paginated separately.

Most periodicals cited in briefs and legal memoranda will be law journals, but occasionally nonlegal, news, or technical publications will be cited.

For citation purposes, do not confuse periodicals with newspapers (which generally are printed on cheaper quality paper, appear in sheet or tabloid form, and contain short articles of recent events, usually unsigned) or loose-leaf services (which consist of unsigned articles and commentaries on specialized subjects, initially filed in a loose-leaf binder, and which later may be collected and bound).

Your first task in citing properly to periodicals is to learn to identify them.

EXERCISE 2

Examine and identify the following publications, for citation purposes, as either a periodical ("P"), newspaper ("N"), or loose-leaf service ("L").

1. The Legal Times   ____
2. Journal of the Patent Office Society   ____
3. BNA Antitrust and Trade Regulation Report   ____
4. Journal of Commerce   ____
5. Barron's   ____
6. National Journal   ____
7. CCH Employment Practices Guide   ____
8. Congressional Quarterly   ____
9. Newsweek   ____
10. Christian Science Monitor   ____

2. Contents

Legal periodicals typically contain some or all of the following types of material (as will be seen, each having its own rules of citation):

(a) Leading Articles. Written by teachers and practitioners. The name of the author is printed in the table of contents and at the beginning of the article.

(b) Student Notes. Written by law students, law review editors, or staff. The name of the author appears (if at all) inconspicuously at the end of the article.

(c) Short Commentary. Brief (unsigned) items on recent cases, legislative developments, newly published books, or specialized bibliographies. These are generally prepared by student contributors.

(d) Signed Book Reviews. Prepared by either student editors or staff or reviewers solicited by the editors.

(e) Special Features. Some issues of a law review may be devoted to a compilation of articles on a single topic, a survey of recent developments in a particular area, or published proceedings of a conference.

3. Author and Title

When citing to a signed article appearing in a periodical, give the author's last name, followed by the title of the article underscored. Follow the capitalization of the cited source. If the cited source prints the title of the article in all capitals, then capitalize the initial word and all other words except articles, conjunctions, and prepositions of four letters or less.

EXAMPLE: Pederson, Formal Records and Informal Rulemaking, 85 Yale L.J. 38 (1975).

(a) Name of Author Omitted. Unsigned articles and materials and notes prepared by students are identified by title only. Descriptive words such as "Note" or "Special Project" appear in regular type preceding the title of the article. (For the correct designation to be

used, consult the table of contents or index to articles appearing in the publication itself.)

EXAMPLE: Note, <u>Last Hired, First Fired Layoffs and Title VII</u>, 88 Harv. L. Rev. 1544 (1975).

(b) Short Title. Certain brief material (such as that prepared by a column editor) is identified, in regular type, by the designation used in the periodical.

EXAMPLE: Book Note, 71 Harv. L. Rev. 395 (1957).

> NOTE: A brief blurb on a book is to be distinguished from a lengthier, signed book review.

(c) Author and Title Omitted. A short commentary on recent developments in the law (such as Recent Decisions and the like) is cited without reference to author or title.

EXAMPLE: 8 U. Chi. L. Rev. 132 (1940).

> NOTE: The reason for this rule is that it would be somewhat illogical to cite a five-year-old case as a "recent decision." Such articles are often appended as commentary to a case citation.

EXAMPLE: <u>Stone v. Powell</u>, 428 U.S. 465 (1976), <u>noted in</u> 30 Vanderbilt L. Rev. 881 (1977).

By way of review:

(1) give *author and full title* when the author is not a student;

(2) give *full title, no author* when the author is a student;

(3) give *short title, no author* when the author is a student and the work is a brief commentary; and

(4) give *no title, no author* when the author is a student and the work is a brief commentary on a recent development in the law.

(d) Case Names in Titles. If a case name appears as part of the title of an article, and the name of the case is italicized in the original, in citing the title of the article, refer to the case name in roman type.

EXAMPLE: Comment, Cost of Notice in Class Action After Oppenheimer Fund, Inc. v. Sanders, 78 Colum. L. Rev. 1517 (1978).

4. Annotations

Annotations (essays on various legal topics) are collected and bound in a series called American Law Reports (A.L.R.). This series was formerly called Lawyer's Reports Annotated (L.R.A.).

Annotations are cited in a manner similar to that of short student material in periodicals. Cite simply "Annot." in roman type, omitting the title of the annotation. The rest of the citation is analogous to a case citation.

EXAMPLE: Annot., 12 A.L.R.2d 282 (1950).

5. Book Reviews

Indicate the last name of the reviewer, followed by "Book Review" in roman type. The title and author of the book being reviewed may be given in parentheses.

EXAMPLE: Koch, Book Review, 22 Antitrust Bull. 723 (1977) (reviewing R. Warren, Antitrust in Theory and Practice (1975).

**Occasionally, a book review may take the form of a titled article. Such reviews should be cited as follows:

EXAMPLE: Calkins, Reply to Professor Leroy L. Lamborn's Book Review of Cases and Materials on Michigan Criminal Law (Book Review), 21 Wayne L. Rev. 1285 (1975).

6. Multiple Authors

When citing to an article written by two or more authors, list each author's last name, in the order listed in the article. The last two names are separated by the symbol "&." Do not shorten to et al.

EXAMPLE: Wagner, Hinz & Vernon, Legal Counsel for the Elderly: Casework, Training and the Aid of Volunteers, 35 NLADA Briefcase 80 (1978).

7. Symposium Articles

Articles within a symposium are cited in the same manner as any other periodical article, without reference to the title of the symposium.

EXAMPLE: Nye, View from the Defense Bar, 22 Antitrust Bull. 267 (1977).

If, however, you wish to cite to the symposium as a whole, list the title of the symposium without reference to any authors. Give the page on which the symposium begins.

EXAMPLE: Legal Aspects of the International Traffic in Stolen Art: A Symposium, 4 Syracuse J. Int'l L. & Com. 51 (1976).

8. Articles in More Than One Part

When citing to articles containing more than one part, indicate the number of parts in parentheses and cite to the first page of each part.

EXAMPLE: Fuller, Legal Fictions (pts. 1–3), 25 Ill. L. Rev. 363, 513, 877 (1930–1931).

If, however, you wish to cite to only one part of a multipart article, list only that part in parentheses and give the first page on which that part begins.

EXAMPLE: Fuller, Legal Fictions (pt. 2), 25 Ill. L. Rev. 513 (1931).

9. Proceedings, Regular Publications by Institutes, and ABA Section Reports

Such materials are cited as periodicals, even though they may be book-length.

EXAMPLE: Cook, Filing Requirements of Regulated Industries, Utilities and Insurance Companies, 1977 N.Y.U. Inst. on Sec. Laws & Regs. 57.

In this example, the volume was not numbered, and so the year was given instead of a volume number. The parenthetical reference to the date was then omitted.

10. Volume Number

How you cite the volume number depends on whether pages are numbered continuously within the volume or separately by issue. If the pages are numbered continuously within the volume, cite the volume number after the title of the article.

EXAMPLE: Lang, Toward a Right to Union Membership, 13 Harv. C.R.–C.L. L. Rev. 31 (1977).

If the pages are numbered separately by issue, omit the volume number and cite as follows:

EXAMPLE: Time, Apr. 12, 1976, at 49.

If no volume number is given, cite the year of publication instead, and omit the date after the page number.

EXAMPLE: 1938 Wis. L. Rev. 281.

11. Name of Periodical

In typewritten briefs and memoranda, the name of the periodical is given in roman type, abbreviated as described following.

**A list of abbreviations for approximately 250 periodicals and single-word components begins on page 92 of the Bluebook. If the title you wish to cite appears in the list, use that form.

EXAMPLE: Current Medicine for Attorneys is cited as "Current Med. for Att'ys."

If the title you wish to cite is not in the list, construct your own abbreviation by looking up each word in the title in this list and (if applicable) in the list of geographical abbreviations on the inside back cover of the Bluebook. For words listed in neither place, use the full word.

After you have determined which abbreviations of main words are to be used, *eliminate* the words "a," "an," "at," "in," "of," and "the" from the title. Abbreviate "and" with the symbol "&." If the name of the periodical includes punctuation marks, *delete* commas and *retain* all other marks.

EXAMPLE: The George Washington Journal of International Law and Economics is abbreviated "Geo. Wash. J. Int'l L. & Econ."

**Following is a partial list of periodical abbreviations that have been changed in the thirteenth edition of the Bluebook:

Chicago[–]Kent Law Review	Chi.[–]Kent L. Rev.
Department of State Bulletin	Dep't St. Bull.
Journal of Criminal Law, Criminology and Police Science	J. Crim. L. Criminology & Police Sci.
Loyola University of Chicago Law Journal	Loy. U. Chi. L.J.

The following list shows frequently encountered words whose abbreviations have been altered in the thirteenth edition:

Counsel	Couns.
Environmental	Envtl.
Foundation	Found.
Library	Libr.
Practitioner	Prac.
Problems	Probs.
Solicitor	Solic.
Taxation	Tax'n
Trust, Trusts	Tr.

12. Spacing

Close up abbreviations consisting of single capital letters.

EXAMPLE: N.Y.L.J.

Do not close up abbreviations consisting of more than one letter.

EXAMPLE: U. Pa. L. Rev.

Do not close up abbreviations when doing so would create a confusing combination with other initials.

EXAMPLE: U.C.L.A. L. Rev.

In the final example, a space is inserted between "U.C.L.A." and "L. Rev." to avoid confusion.

Insert the extra space if a series of single capitals includes three or more consecutive initials that designate an entity that is generally known by these initials (such as "U.C.L.A." and "N.Y.U.").

EXERCISE 3

Using the lists contained in the Bluebook, construct the proper abbreviations for the following periodical titles. Be sure to use the proper spacing.

1. Creighton Law Review   _____

2. University of West Los Angeles Law Review   _____

3. Institute on Securities Regulation   _____

4. Boston College Industrial and Commercial Law Review   _____

5. Fordham Urban Law Journal   _____

6. George Washington Journal of International Law and Economics   _____

7. Trial Lawyer's Quarterly   _____

8. Ottawa Law Review   _____

9. Columbia Journal of Transnational Law   _____

10. Notre Dame Lawyer   _____

13. Page Numbers

When citing to an entire article, give only the page on which the article begins.

EXAMPLE: Note, <u>Civil Commitment of the Mentally Ill</u>, 79 Harv. L. Rev. 1288 (1966).

When wishing to call attention to specific material within an article, cite to the first page of the article and the page or pages on which the specific material appears. The first page and the pinpoint cite are separated by a comma and a space.

EXAMPLE: Note, <u>Municipal Bankruptcy</u>, 84 Yale L.J. 918, 986 (1974).

If you wish to call attention to the first page of an article, repeat the first page number.

EXAMPLE: Note, <u>Municipal Bankruptcy</u>, 84 Yale L.J. 918, 918 (1974).

If the pinpoint cite includes more than one page, give the inclusive page numbers, separated by a hyphen. *Always* retain the last two digits.

EXAMPLE: 4 Mich. L. Rev. 497, 506–08 (1956).
EXAMPLE: 4 Nw. L. Rev. 73, 77–78 (1896).

Do not retain more than two digits unless necessary to show a change in the preceding digit.

EXAMPLE: 88 Harv. L. Rev. 1111–13, 1182–201 (1975).

14. Footnotes

When citing to the content of a footnote, give the page on which the footnote begins, followed by "n." and the footnote number. There is no space between the "n." and the footnote number.

EXAMPLE: 88 Harv. L. Rev. 450, 454 n.20 (1974).

** If the footnote to which you are citing spans more than one page, cite to the page on which the footnote begins when referring to the footnote as a whole.

EXAMPLE: Levine & Levinson, <u>Tax-Free Real Estate Transactions</u>, 9 J. Real Estate Tax'n 151, 153 n.5 (1982).

Otherwise, cite only to the page on which specific material appears.

EXAMPLE: Levine & Levinson, <u>Tax-Free Real Estate Transactions</u>, 9 J. Real Estate Tax'n 151, 154 n.5 (1982).

When citing to a footnote as well as the accompanying text, use the following form:

EXAMPLE: 44 Dick. L. Rev. 31, 33 & n.1 (1939).

The plural of "n." is "nn."

EXAMPLE: 88 Harv. L. Rev. 450, 456 nn.31 & 32 (1974).

15. Date

Ordinarily, the date is cited in parentheses after the page number.

EXAMPLE: 75 Colum. L. Rev. 1233 (1975).

If no volume number appears on the cover or spine of the periodical, however, list the date first, as follows:

EXAMPLE: 1938 Wis. L. Rev. 281.

A different style of citation is employed if each issue of the publication is numbered separately (that is, each new issue begins with page 1). Give the complete date after the title of the periodical, followed by a comma and the page number (preceded by "at" to avoid confusion).

EXAMPLE: Time, Apr. 12, 1976, at 49.

Reason: Since each issue starts with page 1, it is necessary to give the exact date of issue to locate the particular article cited. Periodicals having continuous paging within the volume, on the other hand, would have only one page 49 in each volume, and it would not be necessary to give the date in full in order to locate a particular article.

EXERCISE 4

Assuming that the following citations are accurate, put them into correct citation form.

1. Note: Constitutional Law—first amendment—advertising of prescription drug prices as protected commercial speech. 18 BC Ind. & Com L R 276–317 Ja '77.

2. Gamer, Agent's Privilege to Interfere Intentionally with Contractual Relations: A Reappraisal of California Law, 12 Calif. Western L. Rev. 475, 1976.

3. Civil and Political Rights of Aliens in the U.S.S.R.: A Survey of Soviet Legislation, 11 Texas Int'l. L.J. 571 (1976).

4. Baker, L. John Marshall: A Life in Law. 1974 Am. J. Legal Hist. 20:155 (1976). Reviewed by W.A. Wilbur.

5. Nuclear Power Symposium. 6 Environmental Law 322 (Spring 1976).

6. Bibliography, 9 Journal of Criminal Law. Criminology and Police Science 235 (1955).

7. Annotation, Incorporation in Will of Extrinsic Document Not in Existence at Date of Will, 3 A.L.R. 2d 682 (1949).

8. Sanford Rose, "Checkless Banking Is Bound to Come," Fortune, p. 118, Vol. 95, No. 6 (June 1977).

9. Petersen, R.C., and Stillman, R.C., "Phencyclidine Abuse," Vol. V, Drug Enforcement, p. 19 (July 1978).

10. Special Section—Regulated Industries in Virginia and the 1977 General Assembly, 18 W&M L. Rev. 73 (1976).

C. NEWSPAPERS

As we have seen, the main difference between periodicals and newspapers is the format and the paging. Newspapers are generally printed on cheaper quality paper and appear in unbound sheet or tabloid format. Usually the pages are numbered separately by issue; occasionally they may be numbered consecutively within a volume.

1. Name of Newspaper, Volume

If newspapers are paged continuously within a volume, cite as a periodical.

EXAMPLE: 54 N.Y.L.J. 2017 (1916).

Generally, however, newspapers are cited without reference to volume, and the citation is similar to that of a periodical which is paginated separately by issue.

EXAMPLE: Wash. Post, Feb. 18, 1981, at D8, col. 1.

The name of the newspaper is in regular roman type. Geographical components of names may be abbreviated in the same manner as periodicals. For other words in the name, use the periodical abbreviation list as a guide.

Use caution when abbreviating names of cities. There are many more newspapers in circulation than there are law reviews or other periodicals, so it is advisable to spell out all but the most widely recognized names of cities—even though a particular city (such as Boston) might be abbreviated in a periodical title. With the exception of The London Times (which is cited "The Times (London)"), eliminate "The" from the names of newspapers.

*The names of certain newspapers (Legal Times of Washington, American Lawyer, and the New York Review of Books) are cited in law review footnotes by the Harvard Law Review in the manner of periodicals (that is, in large and small caps), because many law libraries classify these publications as periodicals. The citation is otherwise the same as for newspapers.

2. Date

As shown in these examples, the date is given either parenthetically at the end of the citation (year only) or immediately after the name of the newspaper (exact date), depending on whether the pages are numbered by issue or by volume.

3. Page, Column, and Section

Generally, give the page and column number on which an article begins, preceded by "at." You must include the section number if each section begins with a new page 1.

EXAMPLE: GATT Asked to Settle 13 Trade Disputes in '80, Wall
St. J., Apr. 23, 1981, § 2, at 31, col. 6.

4. Author and Title of Article

**News reports may be cited without title or byline, by title alone,
or by both author and title.

EXAMPLE: Israel Rejects U.S. Rebuke, Wash. Daily News, Feb. 13,
1981, at 16, col. 1.

Cite both the author and title of a signed article other than a news
report. Give the author's last name only.

EXAMPLE: Masters, Tax Havens: Broader Nets Proposed to Catch
Abuses, Legal Times Wash., Feb. 9, 1981, at 2, col. 1.

> NOTE: There is often only a fine distinction between a "news report" and a "signed
> article." Generally, articles of the latter type are analytical as opposed to an item of
> reported fact.

*5. Edition

When citing to the edition appearing in bound or microfilmed
form, there is no need to indicate information concerning the edition
of the newspaper. However, when citing to an edition other than the
one that is bound or microfilmed, indicate that information parenthetically. If you are citing from the newspaper itself and are unsure
which edition is microfilmed, you may likewise include the edition.

EXAMPLE: N.Y. Times, Feb. 17, 1981, at A6, col. 1 (city ed.).

> NOTE: The New York Times is bound in the late city edition.

*6. Cases Cited to Newspapers

Only rarely will a newspaper be the only source available for citing
a case. In such an instance, include in the citation both the date of
publication and the date of decision.

EXAMPLE: Commonwealth v. Ziegler, Legal Intelligencer, Apr. 28,
1981, at 1, col. 2 (Pa. Super. Ct. Apr. 3, 1981).

EXERCISE [5]

Put the following citations into the proper form.

1. Trudeau's Plan to Rewrite Constitution Goes to Canada's Supreme Court Today, by Frederick Rose, The W.S.J., col. 1, p. 15, Apr. 28, 1981.
2. West Africa's Creeping Democracy, by Flora Lewis, The New York Times, p. A23, column 5 (May 4, 1981).
3. Tufaro Transit Co. v. Board of Education of the City of New York (Mar. 11, 1981), in The New York Law Journal, Vol. 185, No. 58 (March. 26, 1981), page 1, col. 6 (S.D.N.Y. Mar. 11, 1981).
4. Democratic Chief Seeks Probe of Right-Wing PACs, The Christian Science Monitor (Eastern ed.), May 6, 1981, at 2, col. 2.
5. Los Angeles Times, September 23, 1979, Part III, page 4, Column 1.

D. Loose-leaf Services

A variety of specialized publications, containing cases, administrative materials, and other reference materials on certain topics, are published in loose-leaf form. Some of these appear as a series of newsletters; others are arranged topically in one or more binders. As particular material is added or updated, new or replacement pages are inserted at appropriate places. Some loose-leaf services are designed to eventually appear in permanently bound form. The name of the publication may change as it is converted from loose-leaf to bound form. Finally, some loose-leafs are kept in semipermanent "transfer binders" prior to being permanently bound.

Loose-leaf services are generally cited in the same manner as other reporters, with the following differences:

(1) the date may be given first, sometimes in brackets;
(2) the name of both the loose-leaf service and bound form may need to be cited;
(3) the name of the publisher is given parenthetically after the name of the service; and
(4) citations may be to paragraph or section numbers, rather than pages.

1. Volume Number

Ordinarily, volumes are numbered and the volume number of the loose-leaf service is given as follows:

EXAMPLE: Hill v. Nacirema Operating Co., 12 Ben. Rev. Bd. Serv. (MB) 119 (Nov. 7, 1979).

> NOTE: This service publishes only decisions of the Benefits Review Board. Therefore, the name of the agency was omitted from the parenthetical.

If no volume number is given, use the year in which the volume is published instead. ** Do not use brackets.

EXAMPLE: Transport Tire Co., 1980–2 B.C.A. (CCH) ¶ 14,586 (1980).

If the case appears in a transfer binder, indicate the inclusive years shown on the spine as follows:

EXAMPLE: Armantrout v. Commissioner, [1975–1979 Transfer Binder] Pens. Plan Guide (CCH) ¶ 22,888 (7th Cir. Feb. 10, 1978).

**The spine of a loose-leaf service may also include a descriptive subtitle, with or without a date or volume number. Cite the name of the service as follows:

EXAMPLE: [Pending Litigation] Envtl. L. Rep. (Envtl. L. Inst.).

EXAMPLE: [2 Drugs Cosmetics] Food Drug Cosm. L. Rep. (CCH).

2. Name of Service

The name of the loose-leaf service follows the volume number or date, abbreviated as shown in the right-hand column of the list beginning on page 109 of the Bluebook.

EXAMPLE: Layne v. Cleland, 24 Empl. Prac. Dec. (CCH) ¶ 31,331 (E.D.N.Y. 1980).

> NOTE: The first entry shown is the name of the loose-leaf; the name of the corresponding bound version, if different, is given in the following line.

> **Names of bound services that are dissimilar to their loose-leaf counterparts are indexed separately and italicized.

Note that in printed briefs and law review articles, the name of the service is printed in large and small capitals for loose-leafs and in regular roman type for bound versions. Also, the citation to loose-leaf services includes the exact date; only the year is given in citations to the bound version. For citation purposes, a transfer binder is treated as a bound service.

* In citing to a loose-leaf service that has not yet been bound, give the name of the bound version in parentheses, if different from the loose-leaf, together with the volume number, if known.

EXAMPLE: Impervious Paint Indus. v. Ashland Oil, 5 Trade Reg. Rep. (CCH) (1980–1 Trade Cas.) ¶ 63,818 (W.D. Ky. Feb. 9, 1981).

If you encounter a service not shown on the list, construct your own abbreviation by analogy to the listed service or periodical abbreviations.

EXAMPLE: Federal Labor Relations Reporter may be abbreviated "Fed. Lab. Rel. Rep."

** Following is a partial list of abbreviations that have been altered in the thirteenth edition of the Bluebook:

Ad. L. Rep. 2d (not Ad. L.2d)
Consumer Cred. Guide (not Cons. Cred. Guide)
Cost Accounting Stand. Guide (not Cost Acc'g Stand. Guide)
Energy Users Rep. (not En. Users Rep.)
Env't Rep. (not Envir. Rep.)
Pub. Util. Rep. (not Pub. U. Rep.)

Note also that names of services, like names of reporters, now abbreviate names of agencies by single initials with periods.

EXAMPLES: E.E.O.C. Compl. Man.
N.Y.S.E. Guide.

3. Publisher

The name of the publisher is given parenthetically after the name of the service, abbreviated as shown in the previously referred to list of abbreviations.

**The name of the publisher may be omitted in citations to bound services. Some of the most commonly encountered publishers are Bureau of National Affairs (BNA), Commerce Clearing House (CCH), Pike & Fischer (P & F), and Prentice-Hall, Inc. (P–H).

EXAMPLE: <u>Brennan v. Aksland</u>, 23 Wage & Hour Cas. (BNA) 484 (E.D. Cal. 1977).

4. Page Number or Subdivision

When citing to a loose-leaf service, use the subdivision designation shown on the list of service abbreviations in the left-hand column. Most services are cited by paragraph number (¶), page number (no symbol), or section number (§). If a case contains both a page number and section or paragraph number, do not confuse the two. Use the designation indicated in the Bluebook. Remember to leave a space between the paragraph or section symbol and the number.

EXAMPLE: <u>Explorer Motor Home Corp. v. Aldridge</u>, [1975–1977 Transfer Binder] Prod. Liab. Rep. (CCH) ¶ 7776 (Tex. Civ. App. 1976).

**If the Bluebook instructs you to cite to "report number," as well as section letter and page, do so as follows:

EXAMPLE: [May 1980 to Apr. 1981] Pat. Trademark & Copyright J. (BNA) No. 524, at A-6 (Apr. 9, 1981).

> NOTE: In this case, the report number of the newsletter is 524, the section letter is A, and the page is 6. The Bluebook also permits a report number to be included if it would assist in locating the cited material. Many of the services published by BNA employ this format.

5. Date

**When citing a case reported in a loose-leaf service, give the exact date. When citing to a bound publication, give the year of decision only.

EXAMPLE: <u>Columbia Broadcasting System v. Image Systems</u>, 16 Cont. Cas. Fed. (CCH) ¶ 80,172 (1971).

In bound publications, if the date has been included in the citation in lieu of the volume number, it is not necessary to repeat the date in parentheses.

EXAMPLE: <u>United States v. Safeway Stores, Inc.</u>, 1970 Trade Cas. (CCH) ¶ 73,257 (N.D. Tex).

Citations to other material appearing in loose-leaf services (such as statutes, regulations, or opinion letters) should include the exact date of promulgation.

EXAMPLE: <u>In re Conner</u>, SEC Accounting Release No. 239, 6 Fed. Sec. L. Rep. (CCH) ¶ 72,261 (Jan. 16, 1978).

If the material cited is undated (such as a short commentary), give the date at the top of the page (for loose-leaf services) or the date of publication (for newsletters).

EXAMPLE: Deering & Fields, <u>Local Courts Clarify the Scope of Protective Orders in L&T Actions</u>, 3 D.C. Real Est. Rep. (Real Est. Rep., Ltd.) 206 (Jan. 1982).

EXERCISE 6

Put the following citations into the proper form.

1. <u>Tumey v. Crown Central Petroleum Corp.</u>, Antitrust Trade Reg. Rep. No. 963 (May 8, 1980), at E-1 (BNA) (Jan.–June 1980 volume).

2. <u>Transcontinental Gas Pipe Line Corp.</u>, Dkt. No. CP78-463, Federal Energy Regulatory Commission Reporter ¶ 62,193 (CCH), Nov. 21, 1980.

3. <u>Pacific Intermountain Express Co. v. Interstate Commerce Commission</u>, 1979 Federal Carriers Cases (9th Cir.), CCH ¶ 82,819 (Feb. 28, 1979).

4. <u>United States Parole Commission v. Gerahty</u>, 26 BNA Crim. Law Rep. 3139 (Mar. 19, 1980).

5. <u>Stauffer Chemical Co. v. FDA</u>, Food, Drug, Cosmetic, L. Rep. (CCH) ¶ 38,065, at p. 38303 (C.D. Cal. 1980).

6. <u>SEC v. Brigadoon Scotch Distributing Co.</u>, 1973 Transfer Binder, CCH Fed. Sec. L. Rep. 94,017 (S.D.N.Y. 1973).

E. OTHER AUTHORITIES

1. Briefs, Motions, Memoranda, and So On

When citing to a brief or pleading from a case, use the designation on the document itself, followed by a reference to the page number and full case citation.

EXAMPLE: Brief for Appellees at 15, Alaska v. Kleppe, No. 76-1829 (D.C. Cir. Feb. 24, 1978).

2. Unpublished Material

Citations for letters, speeches, interviews, dissertations, and other material of limited circulation should be in regular roman type. Give the exact date, if known, in parentheses.

EXAMPLE: Letter from Sidney R. Steele, Chief, Zoning Evaluation Branch, County of Fairfax, Virginia, to Richard C. Deering (Feb. 20, 1981).

EXAMPLE: Address of Stuart Marshall Bloch at Eighth annual conference on Land, Timesharing and the Law, Washington, D.C. (June 15, 1982).

If it is known, include parenthetically information that would help to locate a work, or append a citation to a published source.

EXAMPLE: Telephone conference with Rita Dattola, New York Office of the Attorney General, quoted in Land Trends, Land Dev. L. Rep. (Land Dev. Inst.), Jan. 1982, at 5, col. 2.

*A well-organized law office or library will develop a system for cataloging, indexing, and retrieving materials such as complaints, briefs, motions, legal memoranda or other attorney work products that might be used as an aid in drafting future works. One useful way to catalog such works would be alphabetically by case name. Another method would be to list materials alphabetically by research topic (for example, "Laches," "Strip Mining Legislation"), by type of procedure ("Motion to Suppress Evidence," "Complaint—Personal

Injury," "Petition for Certiorari"), or by jurisdiction (for example, "Eighth Circuit"). For maximum utility, the index could indicate with an asterisk which of the motions and supporting memoranda were ultimately successful. With the advent of word processing equipment, materials may be indexed and located by access words, using any combination of these methods. If word processing is not available, cross indexes may be prepared, or a color-coded labeling scheme could be employed to indicate broad breakdowns such as "Plaintiffs," "Defendants," and "Fifth Circuit." Whatever method is employed, the cite-checker should become familiar with the firm's system so that such materials can be located quickly if necessary.

EXERCISE 7

Put the following citations into the proper form. (If necessary, consult pages 85–86 of the Bluebook.)

1. M. Gottlieb, the Anti-Nazi Boycott Movement in the American Jewish Community 1933–1941, April 1967: unpublished Ph.D. dissertation for Brandeis University, University Microfilm No. 67-16,553.

2. Address by Robert Stipe, Conference on Preservation Law, Washington, D.C. May 1, 1971 (pp. 6–7, unpublished speech).

3. Coalition for Lower Beaufort County v. Alexander, Brief for Appellants, p. 25, No. 77-1866 (U.S. Ct. App. for D.C. Cir., filed 1/26/78).

4. Interview on April 20, 1982 with Stephany Madsen, Managing Editor, Land Development Law Reporter, at the Land Development Institute, Washington, D.C.

5. Remarks of Labor Solicitor Carin Clauss, Conference on Equal Employment and Collective Bargaining, excerpted in BNA's Washington Memorandum, Corporate Practice Series, No. 84, page 1, May 27, 1980.

7 | *Substantive Cite-Checking*

This chapter describes the types and proper use of parentheticals, citations to parallel or related authorities, and introductory signals. It demonstrates when to use citations without a signal and shows the correct order of signals when more than one signal is used, as well as the proper sequence of citations within each signal group. It also illustrates when information about a case may more appropriately be conveyed in a textual discussion than in a parenthetical.

A. PARENTHETICALS

Information on the holding of a case may be conveyed parenthetically immediately following the citation. There are three types of parentheticals: (1) parentheticals indicating the weight of the authority, (2) parentheticals conveying external information about the opinion, and (3) explanatory parentheticals. It is important to understand the differences among the types of parentheticals, because this affects whether they are required and the order in which they are to be given.

1. Parentheticals Indicating Weight of Authority
Whenever a cited proposition is not the single holding of a unani-

mous court, that fact *must* be disclosed parenthetically, to avoid a misleading impression of the impact of the holding on existing case law.

EXAMPLE: The notorious "utterly without redeeming social value" test of obscenity originated in Jacobellis v. Ohio, 378 U.S. 184, 191 (1964), although the language first appeared in Roth v. United States, 354 U.S. 476, 484 (1957) (dictum).[1]

Following is a partial list of parentheticals in this category:

(alternative holding)
(by implication)
(concurring opinion)
(dictum) [i.e., statements not related to direct holding of a case]
(en banc)
(5–4 decision)
(holding unclear)
(MacKinnon, J., concurring in part and dissenting in part)
(per curiam)
(plurality opinion)

**Latin terms such as "per curiam" are no longer italicized.

Such information may generally be verified by examining the beginning or ending of the opinion itself, or by reading the case syllabus or preliminary case summary.

If material within a concurring or dissenting opinion is cited, the citation should include the page on which the case begins and the page on which the cited material appears (not the page on which the separate opinion begins).

EXAMPLE: Even the dissent agreed with the majority in holding that ASCAP's blanket license is not a species of price fixing categorically forbidden by the Sherman Act. Broadcast Music, Inc. v. Columbia Broadcast System, 441 U.S. 1, 25 (1979) (Stevens, J., dissenting).[2]

2. Parentheticals Conveying Other Information

Further information external to the holding itself (such as the author of a majority or plurality opinion) *may* be included in a separate parenthetical.

EXAMPLE: Brandenburg v. Ohio, 395 U.S. 444 (1969) (Douglas, J.).

> NOTE: Authors of concurring and dissenting opinions must be included if the citation refers to that portion of the opinion.

Do not use a parenthetical if the information can be included in the explanatory phrase introducing the authority.

EXAMPLE: Houston Belt & Terminal Ry. Co. v. United States, 153 F. Supp. 3 (S.D. Tex. 1957), aff'd per curiam, 356 U.S. 23 (1958).

3. Explanatory Parentheticals

An explanatory parenthetical (sometimes called a "blurb") summarizes the holding of the case or contains a succinct quotation from the opinion. It may be preceded by a pinpoint cite and is verified by a close reading of the cited portion of the material. Note that parentheticals containing quotations that do not form a complete sentence begin with lower-case letters and that in citations with multiple parentheticals there is a space between parentheticals.

EXAMPLE: The cases decided under the "clear and present danger" theory have all involved threats to national security in some degree. See, e.g., Hess v. Indiana, 414 U.S. 105 (1973) (antiwar demonstration); Brandenburg v. Ohio, 395 U.S. 444 (1969) (per curiam) (threatened march by armed KKK members on Congress); Watts v. United States, 394 U.S. 705 (1969) (per curiam) (threatening the life of the president of the United States); Bond v. Floyd, 385 U.S 116 (1966) (individuals who burned draft cards as an antiwar protest); Scales v. United States, 367 U.S. 203 (1961) (Communist Party advocating violent revolution and overthrow of the government); Abrams v. United States, 250 U.S. 616 (1919) (encouraging resistance to the war effort).[3]

EXAMPLE: The doctrine of free speech has been attributed to Justice Brandeis' oft-quoted concurring opinion in Whitney v. California, 274 U.S. 357, 378 (1927) ("The fact that speech is likely to result in some violence or destruction of property is not enough to justify its suppression.").[4]

If the information cannot be conveyed briefly in a parenthetical, it may be preferable to disclose the information textually, outside of the citation.

EXAMPLE: In Pittsburgh Press Co. v. Pittsburgh Comm'n on Human Relations, 413 U.S. 376 (1973), the Court rejected the newspaper's argument that its decision to place these want ads under the categories of "Jobs—Male Interest" and "Jobs—Female Interest" was editorial and thus protected by the First Amendment. Id. at 386. The Court held not only that the advertisements were "classic examples of commercial speech," id. at 385, and thus entitled to less weight in a First Amendment analysis, but also that "[d]iscrimination in employment is...illegal commercial activity." Id. at 388 (emphasis in original).[5]

**Similar information may be appended to any other type of authority.

EXAMPLE: H.R. Rep. No. 1104, 96th Cong., 2d Sess. 190 (1980) (renegotiation of agreements under Defense Production Act Amendments interpreted by conferees to contemplate "mutual consent").

EXERCISE [1]

In the following case citations, verify the information contained in the parenthetical. If no parenthetical is given, add one, if necessary. If quotations are given, verify the quote and the pinpoint cite. If a case summary is given, edit the summary or recast as a separate discussion if you feel it appropriate.

1. Watts v. United States, 394 U.S. 705 (1969).
2. See also Thornhill v. Alabama, 310 U.S. 88, 102–03 (1940) (purely informational union picketing entitled to constitutional protection.)[6]
3. See United States v. South-Eastern Underwriters Ass'n, 322 U.S. 553, 533–60 (1944) (insurance industry fell within ambit of the

Sherman Act even though the Court had ruled prior to 1980 that insurance was not commerce and therefore was subject to court regulation).[7]

4. The Court subsequently elaborated on its definition of boycott in terms of commercial objectives in St. Paul Fire & Marine Insurance Co. v. Barry, 438 U.S. 531, 543–44 (1978) (the Sherman Act held to apply where plaintiff has induced its competitors to refuse to deal on any terms with its customers in order to keep policyholders from obtaining alternative sources of coverage and even from negotiating for more favorable terms elsewhere; although the boycotters and their targets were not involved in competitive relationships with each other, the Sherman Act was still violated because of the horizontal agreement among the parties to stop selling to particular customers).[8]

5. Another case in which the Court has recognized that expressive conduct is protected under the first amendment is Eisenstadt v. Baird, 405 U.S. 438, 455, 460 (1972) (Justice Douglas, concurring).

B. RELATED AUTHORITIES

1. Treatment of Principal Authority by Related Authority

A source that reprints, discusses, or quotes from the principal authority may be added to the citation, introduced by an italicized explanatory phrase as shown in the following example.

EXAMPLE: A. Trebach, The Rationing of Justice 83, 264 (1964), quoted in Note, Constitutional Limitations on the Conditions of Pretrial Detention, 79 Yale L.J. 941, 941 n.2 (1970).

Examples of other introductory words that may be used to bring in such secondary authorities follow:

cited with approval in	noted in
construed in	questioned in
criticized in	quoted in
discussed in	reviewed in

2. Treatment of Related Authority by Principal Authority

If a principal authority discusses or quotes from a related authority, you may indicate that fact parenthetically as follows. Note that the introductory words are not italicized.

EXAMPLE: Nimmer, The Meaning of Symbolic Speech Under the First Amendment, 21 U.C.L.A. L. Rev. 29, 42–43 (1973) (discussing Tinker v. Des Moines Independent School District, 393 U.S. 503 (1969)).

3. Order of Citation

If more than one parenthetical or related authority is given in a citation, arrange the components of the citation in the following order:

1. Basic citation (which generally includes a parenthetical containing the date).
2. Parentheticals indicating weight of authority.
3. Parentheticals giving other information.
4. Explanatory parentheticals.
5. Sources reprinting the main authority.
6. Prior or subsequent history.
7. Related authority—discussed in, quoted in, and so on.

EXAMPLE: Mars v. United States, 463 F. Supp. 87, 90–94 (E.D. Mich. 1978) (refusing to give retroactive application to United States v. Mauro), aff'd, 615 F.2d 704 (6th Cir.), cert. denied, 449 U.S. 849 (1980), noted in Annot., 98 A.L.R. 3d 160, 252 n.9 (1980).

In the preceding example, note that the explanatory parenthetical is appended to the opinion from which it is derived.

C. USE OF CITATIONS TO SUPPORT STATEMENTS MADE IN TEXT

We have now learned what is included in a complete citation to many types of authorities. The remainder of this chapter will show the relationship between a statement made in the text (called a "proposition") and the authorities cited in support of that statement.

When cite-checking a brief or memo, be alert to the fact that every assertion in the text must be supported by one or more authorities. If no authority is cited, the author should be asked to provide one. Citations to authorities may be made directly or they may be preceded by an appropriate introductory signal that characterizes the degree of support the citations give to the statement made. Mastery of these signals is essential for precise and effective legal writing.

1. Citation Without a Signal

A direct citation to a case or other authority without the use of an introductory signal is appropriate whenever the cited case directly supports a statement made in the text, identifies the source of a quotation, or identifies an authority referred to in the text.

EXAMPLE: In 1978, the Court suggested that it might reexamine the scope of the per se rule with respect to group boycotts. St. Paul Fire & Marine Insurance Co. v. Barry, 438 U.S. 531 (1978).[9]

EXAMPLE: The Court, in reversing the court of appeals' conclusions with respect to the per se illegality of the blanket license, explained that "[e]asy labels do not always supply ready answers." Broadcast Music, Inc. v. Columbia Broadcasting System, 441 U.S. 1, 8 (1979).[10]

EXAMPLE: The Court in 1977 overruled the per se rule against vertical territorial and customer restraints embodied in the Schwinn doctrine. Continental T.V., Inc. v. GTE Sylvania, Inc., 433 U.S. 36 (1977) (overruling United States v. Arnold, Schwinn & Co., 388 U.S. 365 (1967)).[11]

2. Introductory Signals

If a cited case gives anything other than unqualified support for the statement made, it should be preceded by the appropriate introductory signal. This section provides a list of signals along with explanations of their proper use. Substantive cite-checking should include evaluation of whether the proper signal was used. If anything other than the precise word or phrases shown in the following is used, the signal should be revised accordingly. The signal should be followed by the punctuation mark shown here.

(a) Signals That Indicate Support (positive signals). The following signals are appropriate whenever the cited authority supports the statement in a qualified manner. The signals are listed in descending order of the degree of support they offer.

(1) E.g.,—The cited authority is one of several examples that could be given in support of the proposition.

EXAMPLE: A minority of courts have refused to be guided by the presumption of innocence in determining a detainee's rights during pretrial confinement. E.g., Bell v. Wolfish, 441 U.S. 520, 533 (1979); Feeley v. Sampson, 570 F.2d 364, 367 (1st Cir. 1978); Hampton v. Holmesburg Prison Officials, 546 F.2d 1077, 1080 n.1 (3d Cir. 1976).[12]

NOTE: E.g., preceded by a comma, may also be used in combination with other signals.

EXAMPLE: Most states in their scheme of unemployment benefit determination provide for the issuance of subpoenas ad testificandum or duces tecum to gather evidence for the determination hearing. See, e.g., Cal. Unemp. Ins. Code § 1953 (West 1972); Ill. Ann. Stat. ch. 48, § 500 (Smith-Hurd 1980); Mich. Comp. Laws Ann. § 421.9 (West 1978).[13]

(2) Accord—Accord is used to introduce a second authority or line of authorities after one authority has been cited in direct support of the statement made. The use of this signal is particularly apt when citation to a leading authority without a signal is accompanied by a quotation from that case. An additional authority that also supports the proposition is then introduced by accord, to make clear that the quotation is being attributed to the first authority cited.

EXAMPLE: Some state constitutions have no provision analogous to the federal equal protection clause. The courts of those states review nonuniform economic regulations under clauses stating that the legislature "shall not grant to any citizen or class of citizens privileges or immunities which upon the same terms shall not equally belong to all citizens." Ark. Const. art. II, § 18; accord, e.g., Cal. Const. art. I, § 7.[14]

Accord is also used to introduce the law of another jurisdiction which is in agreement with the law of the jurisdiction previously cited.

EXAMPLE: In a recent Eighth Circuit case it was held that the purchaser's reserved right to terminate the vendor's management agreement would render the buyer's role "significant" and hence the transaction was not an investment contract. Fargo Partners v. Dain Corp., 540 F.2d 912, 915 (8th Cir. 1976); accord Andrews v. Blue, 489 F.2d 367, 374–75 (10th Cir. 1973) (percentage in real estate venture held an investment contract where designation of plaintiff as a "consultant" was in name only).

**No comma appears after this signal.

(3) See—The cited authority supports the proposition for which it is cited. However, the statement is *not* made directly in the cited authority but logically follows from it. (This signal is often incorrectly used when no signal should be used.)

See may properly be used, for example, when the text of the brief or memorandum states a conclusion that is supported by statistics contained in the cited authorities.

EXAMPLE: Although nonbanking firms normally consummate mergers quickly in order to minimize disruption of their business, the agency approval process typically delays consummation of even small bank mergers for several months. See, e.g., First American National Bank of St. Cloud, Comptroller of the Currency, 1979 Annual Report 58 (Nov. 21, 1979) (banks reached merger agreement Jan. 31, 1979; application filed Apr. 5, 1979, approved Nov. 21, 1979); Wells Fargo Bank, Nat'l Ass'n, Comptroller of the Currency, 1979 Annual Report 101 (June 14, 1979) (agreement reached Sept. 27, 1978; application filed Feb. 27, 1979, approved June 14, 1979).[15]

(4) <u>See also</u>—The cited authority constitutes additional material in support of the cited proposition, which cannot be included with a preceding group of authorities because of some variation from the original proposition.

**The use of a parenthetical explanation in conjunction with this signal is "strongly recommended."

EXAMPLE: Nine states have antimonopoly provisions in their constitutions that can be used analogously to economic due process in price-fixing and entry barrier cases. <u>See</u> Ark. Const. art. II, § 19; Ga. Const. art. III, § VIII, para. VIII; Md. Const. Declaration of Rights, art. 41; N.H. Const. pt. 2, art. 83; N.C. Const. art. I, § 34; Okla. Const. art. II, § 32; Tenn. Const. art. I, § 22; Tex. Const. art. I, § 26; Wyo. Const. art. I, § 30; <u>see also</u> <u>In re Aston Park Hospital, Inc.</u>, 282 N.C. 542, 193 S.E.2d 729 (1973) (antimonopoly clause alternative ground for invalidating certificate-of-need requirement for private hospital).[16]

(5) <u>Cf.</u>—The signal <u>cf.</u> is derived from the Latin <u>conferre</u>, to compare. It is used whenever the cited authority supports a different proposition from the one made in text, but the different proposition is sufficiently analogous to lend support to the statement make in text. **An explanatory parenthetical should accompany <u>cf.</u> to show in what respect the holding of the cited authority differs from the given proposition.

EXAMPLE: At least one court has refused to extend federal question jurisdiction over a state party without some positive indication of congressional intent. <u>See</u> <u>Long Prairie Parking Co. v. Midwest Emery Freight System</u>, 429 F. Supp. 201, 203–04 (D. Mass. 1977); <u>cf.</u> <u>Alexander v. Gardner-Denver Co.</u>, 415 U.S. 36, 48 & n.9 (1974) (congressional intent behind title VII requires that an individual pursue his federal and state remedies independently, even though federal courts have exclusive jurisdiction over the federal claim).[17]

(b) Signals That Suggest a Useful Comparison (comparative signals: Compare...with...; compare...and...with...and...). This signal is appropriate when a case or group of cases is to be contrasted with a second line of cases as support for a statement made in text. The difference between cf. and compare is that cf. introduces authorities that support the proposition, albeit by analogy, whereas compare introduces sources neither of which alone can support the statement made in the text, and which therefore must be read together.

EXAMPLE: Prior to the promulgation of the 1978 guidelines, a conflict had arisen as to whether the criterion-related method of validation was legally required whenever feasible to the exclusion of other methods. Compare Kirkland v. New York State Department of Correctional Services, 520 F.2d 420, 426 (2d Cir. 1975) (upholding district court's requirement that defendant's employment tests be validated on basis of content or construct) with Vulcan Society v. Civil Service Commission, 490 F.2d 387, 394–95 (2d Cir. 1973) (rejecting plaintiff's contention that examinations must be validated by predictive or concurrent method).[18]

In a compare cite, the connectives "with" and "and" are preceded by a comma *unless* the citation immediately preceding the connective contains no commas at all.

EXAMPLE: Compare supra note 56 with infra note 91. [No commas.]

EXAMPLE: Compare Kirkland v. New York State Department of Correctional Services, 520 F.2d at 426, with Vulcan Society v. Civil Service Commission, 490 F.2d at 394–95. [Comma precedes "with."]

(c) Signals That Indicate Contradiction (negative signals). Frequently, a discussion in a brief will reveal a split of opinion in a disputed area of the law. The following group of signals are used to introduce authorities whose holdings contradict the main proposition.

(1) <u>Contra</u>—<u>Contra</u> is used when the cited authority directly contradicts a statement made in the text. It is the equivalent of no signal in support of a statement made. ** No comma is used after this signal.

EXAMPLE: The failure of <u>Miller</u> to increase the conviction rate is seen by one commentator as following ineluctably from the fact that public attitudes about sex have become increasingly liberal. E. Kronhausen & P. Kronhausen, <u>Pornography and the Law</u> 291 (1959). <u>Contra</u> George, <u>Obscenity Litigation: An Overview of Currently Legal Controversies</u>, 3 Nat'l J. Crim. Def. 189 (1977). This commentator argues that <u>Miller</u> greatly reduced the prosecutor's burden and, in effect, encouraged wider state efforts to regulate obscenity.[19]

**(2) <u>But see</u>—<u>But see</u> is used when the cited authority <u>directly contradicts</u> a stated proposition. It is the counterpart of <u>see</u> used to support a positive statement made.

EXAMPLE: Recently, the Court explicitly rejected the "beyond a reasonable doubt" standard in criminal cases, in favor of presumptions that are permissive rather than mandatory. <u>County Court of Ulster County, New York. v. Allen</u>, 442 U.S. 140 (1979). <u>But see</u> <u>Tot v. United States</u>, 319 U.S. 463, 467–68 (1943) (holding that to meet due process requirements, there must be a "rational connection between the fact proved and the ultimate fact presumed").[20]

(3) <u>But cf.</u>—The cited authority supports a proposition analogous to the *opposite* of the position stated in the text. ** As in the case of <u>cf.</u>, the use of an explanatory parenthetical is "strongly recommended."

EXAMPLE: Under the Bank Merger Act of 1966, private plaintiffs challenging an agency approval are entitled to de novo review in the courts under the same provisions that apply to suits by the Attorney General. 12 U.S.C.

§ 1828(c)(7)(1976); see Southwest Mississippi Bank v. FDIC, 499 F. Supp. 1, 5–8 (S.D. Miss. 1979) (dictum), aff'd mem., 625 F.2d 1013 (5th Cir. 1980). But cf. First Midland Bank & Trust v. Chemical Financial Corp., 441 F. Supp. 414, 421–23 (W.D. Mich. 1977) (construing statute to require separate procedural treatment of private party suits under both Bank Merger Act of 1966 and Bank Holding Company Act of 1956).[21]

(d) Signals That Introduce Background Material.

(1) See generally— The cited authority provides helpful background material related to the issue under discussion. This signal is often used to direct the reader to law review articles. **The use of an explanatory parenthetical in conjunction with this signal is "encouraged."

EXAMPLE: Determining whether the withholding of patronage from the boycott target is an activity protected by the first amendment requires an analysis under the evolving "symbolic speech" doctrine. See generally Nimmer, The Meaning of Symbolic Speech Under the First Amendment, 21 U.C.L.A. L. Rev. 23 (1973) (discussing the genesis of the doctrine).[22]

**(e) Use of Signals as Verbs.

In some discussions, certain signal words such as "see," "compare," or "see generally" are used simply as verbs of sentences and not in their signal sense. In such sentences, the words should be printed in regular roman type. There should be no explanatory parentheticals in sentences of this type; rather, the sentence itself may contain a discussion of the case holding.

EXAMPLE: See generally Republic Steel Corp. v. NLRB, 311 U.S. 7 (1940), and UAW v. Russell, 356 U.S. 634 (1958), in which the Court found the award of punitive damages to be beyond the authority of the NLRB.[23]

EXAMPLE: When cost-free information concerning prices is not readily available and marketplaces are differentiated, the price of a homogeneous commodity in a given market-place may be strikingly higher than the price at which the commodity is normally sold. See, e.g., On Fifth Avenue, Shoppers' Jungle, N.Y. Times, July 9, 1980, at C1, col. 5. For further data, see the companion article, 'Good Price' Proves To Be No Bargain, N.Y. Times, July 9, 1980, at C9, col. 1.[24]

EXERCISE 2

In the following exercises, examine the authorities cited and evaluate whether the appropriate signal was used. Revise the signals used to introduce the citations if necessary.

1. For an extensive discussion of the difficulties inherent in regulating carcinogens and the consequent necessity of making policy choice, see McGarity, Substantive and Procedural Discretion in Administrative Resolution of Science Policy Questions: Regulating Carcinogens in EPA and OSHA, 67 Geo. L. J. 729 (1979).[25]

2. The term "under color of law" was initially interpreted to mean that the plaintiff must demonstrate that his or her constitutional rights were violated pursuant to the enforcement of a statute or ordinance. See Hague v. C.I.O., 307 U.S. 496 (1939) (city ordinance prohibited public meetings and distribution of printed materials); Lane v. Wilson, 307 U.S. 268 (1939) (damages awarded to blacks who were denied the right to vote by a discriminatory state statute).[26]

3. In general, where other actions have not been commenced, class action treatment is deemed proper. See generally also, e.g., Hohmann v. Packard Instrument Co., 399 F.2d 711 (7th Cir. 1968); Fidelis Corp. v. Litton Industries, 293 F. Supp. 164, 171 (S.D.N.Y. 1968).[27].

4. The Clean Water Act allows an aggrieved state to bring a direct action against the administrator for failure to enforce federal or state discharge requirements in a neighboring state. Compare Illinois v. City of Milwaukee, 406 U.S. 91, 107 (1972).[28]

5. There is a split among the circuits as to whether the federal common-law nuisance doctrine is applicable to actions brought under the Clean Water Act. Evansville v. Kentucky Liquid Recycling Corp., 604 F.2d 1008, 1016 (7th Cir. 1979). But cf., National Sea

Clammers Ass'n v. City of New York, 616 F.2d 1222 (3d Cir. 1980), where the Third Circuit upheld an implied private right of action under the Clean Water Act.[29]

3. Structure of Citations

Citations immediately follow the statement they support. If they support only portions of a statement made, they are to be inserted into the middle of the sentence and set off by commas. Do not use a comma to precede a citation to a sentence as a whole.

EXAMPLE: Since its initial enactment, title VII of the Civil Rights Act of 1964 has been fortified by legislative amendment. See Equal Employment Opportunity Act of 1972, Pub. L. No. 92–261, 86 Stat 103 (amending 42 U.S.C. §§ 2000e to 2000e–15 (1964)).[30]

EXAMPLE: As it had in Illinois v. Milwaukee, 599 F.2d 151 (7th Cir. 1979), the court rejected pendent state law claims as independent causes of action. Evansville v. Kentucky Liquid Recycling Corp., 604 F.2d 1008, 1016 (7th Cir. 1979).[31]

If a citation consists of multiple authorities, separate the individual authorities cited by semicolons.

EXAMPLE: See Penn Central Transportation Co. v. City of New York, 438 U.S. 104 (1978); Village of Arlington Heights v. Metro Housing Corp., 429 U.S. 252 (1977); Young v. American Mini Theatres, 427 U.S. 50 (1976); Village of Belle Terre v. Boraas, 416 U.S. 1 (1974).[32]

D. ORDER OF CITATIONS

1. Order of Signals

When more than one signal is used to introduce various authorities, the signals should be listed in the order shown previously. Thus, signals showing positive support (together with the authorities they introduce) will be given before signals showing contradictory holdings, and signals introducing background materials will always go last.

If the citations used are introduced by signals of the same type (i.e., positive, comparative, negative, or background) they may be strung together within a single clause or sentence, separated by semicolons.

EXAMPLE: Rule 23(b)(3)(A)–(D) lists four factors that are pertinent to the findings of predominance and superiority. These four factors are nonexhaustive and do not preclude the court from considering other factors relevant to a determination of predominance and superiority. Kamm v. California City Development Co., 509 F.2d 205, 212 (9th Cir. 1975); Mitchell v. Texas Gulf Sulphur Co., 446 F.2d 90, 107 (10th Cir. 1971); Clayton v. Skelly Oil Co., 26 Fed. R. Serv. 2d (Callaghan) 317, 320 (S.D.N.Y. 1978); cf. Katz v. Carte Blanche Corp., 496 F.2d 747, 760 (3d Cir.) (listing points of view from which superiority must be scrutinized), cert. denied, 419 U.S. 885 (1974); Green v. Wolf Corp., 406 F.2d 291, 301 (2d Cir. 1968) (relevant question is number of members in proposed class), cert. denied, 395 U.S. 977 (1969).[33]

If, however, signals of different types are used, each grouping of citations introduced by a different signal must form a new sentence.

EXAMPLE: A recent decision of the Supreme Court held that the mere fact that title to federal lands is involved does not create a federal question; state law must be inadequate or inconsistent with federal policy. Miree v. DeKalb County, 433 U.S. 25 (1977) (state law generally controls dealings of private parties in an oil and gas lease issued under the federal Mineral Leasing Act); see also Wallis v. Pan-American Petroleum Corp., 384 U.S. 63, 71 (1966). Contra Illinois v. City of Milwaukee, 599 F.2d 151, 162 (7th Cir. 1979) (action based on federal common-law nuisance doctrine; state's more stringent limitations held "fully consistent" with the federal Water Pollution Control Act).[34]

2. Order of Authorities Within a Signal

When a given signal is used to introduce several authorities, these sources must be arranged in a precise order, based on the strength of support offered. (In general, a higher court offers stronger support than a lower court; a more recent pronouncement has more weight than an older one.) When determining the order of case citations, look to the first decision cited; disregard the subsequent or prior history.

Within each of the following categories, if more than one type of authority is listed all such sources are treated as the same level. (For example, it is not necessary to separate appellate opinions by circuit; all federal appellate decisions are grouped together and listed by date, most recent case first.) If the short form of a source is used, it will be necessary to check the date by reference to the first citation.

The Bluebook contains, on pages 11–13, a master list indicating the proper order of authorities within signals. Following is a partial reproduction of that list.

1. Federal court decisions (arranged in reverse chronological order, most recent case first, within the following categories):
   (*a*) Supreme Court
   (*b*) Circuit courts of appeal, emergency court of appeals, and temporary emergency court of appeals
   (*c*) District courts
   (*d*) Court of Claims
** (*e*) Other federal courts: Court of Customs and Patent Appeals, Court of International Trade, Court of Military Appeals, Customs Court, Railroad Reorganization Court, Tax Court, Board of Tax Appeals
** (*f*) Bankruptcy appellate panels and judges
2. Opinions of federal administrative agencies (arranged alphabetically by agency, most recent case first)
3. Decisions of state courts (arranged alphabetically by state; within state, higher courts listed first; within each court, most recent case listed first)
4. Decisions of state agencies (arranged alphabetically by state; within state, listed alphabetically by agency)
**5. Constitutions (U.S., followed by state constitutions, alphabetically by state)

6. Federal statutes, in the following order:
   (*a*) Statutes in U.S.C., U.S.C.A., or U.S.C.S. (cited in forward order of U.S.C. title)
   (*b*) Statutes in force but not yet in U.S.C., U.S.C.A., or U.S.C.S. (most recent enactments cited first)
** (*c*) Federal rules of evidence and procedure
   (*d*) Statutes no longer in force (most recent enactments cited first)
7. State statutes, in the following order (arranged alphabetically by state):
   (*a*) Statutes cited to the current codification (by order in the codification)
   (*b*) Statutes in force but not yet codified (most recent enactments first)
** (*c*) Rules of evidence and procedure
   (*d*) Repealed statutes (most recent enactment first)
**8. Legislative materials (most recent first):
   (*a*) Bills and resolutions
   (*b*) Committee hearings
   (*c*) Congressional reports, documents, and committee prints
   (*d*) Congressional debates
9. Federal administrative regulations, arranged separately as follows:
   (*a*) Executive orders
   (*b*) Current Treasury regulations
   (*c*) Proposed Treasury regulations
   (*d*) Other federal agency regulations (cited in order of C.F.R. title)
   (*e*) All repealed federal regulations
10. State administrative regulations (arranged alphabetically by state):
   (*a*) Currently in force
   (*b*) Repealed
11. Records
12. Briefs
13. Petitions
14. Secondary authorities:
   (*a*) Books, pamphlets, and collected essays of a single author (alphabetically by author; if no author, then alphabetically by title)

(*b*) Signed periodical articles and collected essays of various authors (alphabetically by author)

(*c*) Student-written law review material (arranged alphabetically by periodical, as abbreviated), in the following order:
(1) Special student projects
(2) Student notes
(3) Short commentary on recent developments

(*d*) Signed book reviews (alphabetically by reviewer)

(*e*) Student-written book notes (alphabetically by periodical)

** (*f*) Newspaper articles (most recent first)

** (*g*) Annotations (most recent first)

** (*h*) Unpublished material and other material of limited circulation (alphabetically by author; if no author, then by first word of title)

*This organization scheme may be varied "for any good reason." One possible variation might be to separate appellate decisions by circuit or to list decisions of a particular district court first. Such a scheme might be appropriate when discussing a split of opinion among the circuits or when discussing a trend within a particular jurisdiction.

**If a certain authority is considered more significant than other authorities cited within the signal, it should be listed first, regardless of its classification.

In the following examples, the authorities are correctly arranged according to the outline shown previously.

EXAMPLE: See Poelker v. Doe, 432 U.S. 519 (1977); Maher v. Roe, 432 U.S. 464 (1977); Beal v. Doe, 432 U.S. 438 (1977). See also Zbaraz v. Quern, 596 F.2d 196 (7th Cir. 1979); Preterm, Inc. v. Dukakis, 591 F.2d 121 (1st Cir. 1979); Roe v. Ferguson, 515 F.2d 279 (6th Cir. 1975); Doe v. Rose, 499 F.2d 1112 (10th Cir. 1974); Klein v. Nassau County Medical Center, 409 F. Supp. 731 (E.D.N.Y. 1976) (per curiam), vacated and remanded, 433 U.S. 902 (1977) (in light of Beal v. Doe and Maher v. Roe); Roe v. Norton, 408 F. Supp. 660 (D. Conn. 1975); Coe v. Hooker, 406 F. Supp. 1072 (D.N.H. 1976); Doe v. Rampton, 366 F. Supp. 189 (D. Utah 1973).[35]

EXAMPLE: Most works on the subject have concluded that the leg-
islative history indicates that title IX of the Organized
Crime Control Act of 1970 is directed toward preventing
the infiltration of legitimate businesses only. Bradley,
Racketeers, Congress, and the Courts: An Analysis of
RICO, 65 Iowa L. Rev. 837 (1980); McClellan, The
Organized Crime Control Act (S. 30) or Its Critics:
Which Threatens Civil Liberties?, 46 Notre Dame Law.
55 (1970); Comment, Title IX of the Organized Crime
Control Act of 1970: An Analysis of Issues Arising in Its
Interpretation, 27 De Paul L. Rev. 89 (1977); Comment,
Organized Crime and the Infiltration of Legitimate Busi-
ness: Civil Remedies for "Criminal Activity," 124 U.
Pa. L. Rev. 192 (1975); Note, Elliott v. United States:
Conspiracy Law and the Judicial Pursuit of Organized
Crime Through RICO, 65 Va. L. Rev. 109 (1979).[36]

EXERCISE [3]

Assume that all authorities shown in these groups follow a single
signal. In the blanks to the right, indicate in the space provided the
correct order within the signal.

1. Sindell v. Abbott Laboratories, 26 Cal. 3d 588, 607 P.2d
924, 163 Cal. Rptr. 132, cert. denied, 101 S. Ct. 285 (1980).   _____
2. 3B J. Moore, Moore's Federal Practice ¶ 23.60, at
469–70 (2ded. 1980).   _____
3. 29 C.F.R. § 1910.1028 (1979).   _____
4. S. Rep. No. 1282, 91st Cong., 2d Sess. 4, reprinted in
1970 U.S. Code Cong. & Ad. News 5177, 5180.   _____
5. 122 Cong. Rec. H8632 (daily ed. Aug. 10, 1976) (re-
marks of Rep. Abzug).   _____
6. McRae v. Califano, 491 F. Supp. 630 (E.D.N.Y. 1980).   _____
7. Anders v. California, 386 U.S. 738 (1967).   _____
8. Comment, Federal Court Stays and Dismissals in Def-
erence to Parallel State Court Proceedings: The Impact of
Colorado River, 44 U. Chi. L. Rev. 641, 644 (1977).   _____
9. Clark v. Watchie, 513 F.2d 994 (9th Cir.), cert. denied,
423 U.S. 841 (1975).   _____

10. Mowrey, Attorney Fees in Securities Class Action and Derivative Suits, 34 J. Corp. L. 267, 269–70 (1977).   _____

EXERCISE 4

The following exercises consist of several signals, each followed by one or more authorities. Assuming that the cited sources are intro-duced by the appropriate signal, rearrange the citations by indicating in the space provided the correct sequence, so that both the correct order of signals and the correct order of authorities within signal groups are followed.

1. See also
   - (a) Annot., 51 A.L.R.3d 1444 (1973).   _____
   - (b) Restatement (Second) of Torts § 402A, comment c (1965).   _____
   - (c) O'Connell, Expanding No-Fault Beyond Auto In-surance: Some Proposals, 59 Va. L. Rev. 749, 773 (1973).   _____
   - (d) Comment, Tests for Discrimination in Employ-ment, 28 Wash. & Lee L. Rev. 194 (1971).   _____

2. See
   - (a) Cal. Const. art. 13a, §§ 1–6.   _____
   - (b) Los Angeles Daily J., Feb. 19, 1980, at 1, col. 3.   _____
   - (c) J. Rawls, A Theory of Justice (1971).   _____
   - (d) Act of Oct. 30, 1972, Pub. L. No. 92–603 § 249F, 86 Stat. 1329, 1429.   _____
   - (e) People v. Leyra, 302 N.Y. 353, 98 N.E.2d 553 (1951).   _____

3. But see
   - (a) Note, The Polygraphic Technique: A Selective Analysis, 20 Drake L. Rev. 330, 330–31 (1971).   _____
   - (b) Summers, Pragmatic Instrumentalism: America's Leading Theory of Law, 5 Cornell L. Rev. 15 (1978).   _____
   - (c) International Brotherhood of Teamsters v. United States, 431 U.S. 324 (1977).   _____
   - (d) Laffey v. Northwest Airlines, 567 F.2d 429 (D.C. Cir. 1976).   _____

(*e*)	Andrew Dossett Imports, Inc. v. United States, 273 F. Supp. 908 (Cust. Ct. 1967).	____

(*f*)	Fitzsimmons v. Greater St. Louis Sports Enterprises, 63 F.R.D. 620 (S.D. Ill. 1974).	____

8 | *Putting a Brief into Final Form*

This chapter contains a checklist of items to be handled after the final draft of a brief or memorandum has been prepared, so that the final product is internally consistent. It describes how to set up a table of contents and table of authorities and gives examples of each. It reviews the steps involved in assembling an appendix and complying with court requirements set forth in Chapter 1.

A. FINAL DETAILS IN TEXT

Once the text of a brief or memo has been revised and all the citations have been checked and put into the proper form, the next step is to proofread the revised draft to make sure that all the requested changes were made and that no new errors were made in any retyped portion. If word processing is used, familiarize yourself with the characteristics of the equipment so that you can be alert to any potential problems involved in the retyping (such as a tendency to drop hyphens at the end of a line).

Before handing the last draft to the typist, it is also a good idea to look over the text one more time and make sure the following items are in order.

1. Internal Consistency

Make sure that each time an authority is cited, it is cited the same way. This is particularly important if you have picked up an error in an earlier draft. (If an authority is cited numerous times, adopting the appropriate short form of citation will reduce the possibility of inconsistent citations.)

2. New Material Added

If a memo has been through several drafts, and additional authorities have been inserted at various points, surrounding references may have to be changed. Be particularly careful of intervening citations added to an extensive discussion of a single authority, containing numerous occurrences of "id." Similarly, if the initial reference to a particular authority has been deleted or rearranged, subsequent references may have to be rewritten in full.

3. Footnotes

If footnotes are used, be sure that for every reference in text to a footnote there is a corresponding footnote. It is a good idea to save all prior drafts until the memo has been put into final form, in case it is necessary to trace back a dropped footnote or eliminate one that should have been dropped. It is far easier to reconstruct footnotes from drafts than to recheck the sources themselves. If the text contains a reference to a numbered footnote and the footnotes have been renumbered, it will be necessary to change the footnote references as well. Some word-processing systems are capable of renumbering footnotes automatically; however, you should be alert to mechanical errors, such as dropped or repeated lines.

4. Internal Cross References

If the brief or memorandum refers to other parts of itself, be aware that the page numbers are likely to change if extensive changes are made, and thus cross references may be affected. One way to avoid the time-consuming process of double-checking each cross reference (and to eliminate the possibility of overlooking a reference) is to purposely leave such references blank until the draft is near completion. Another method is to cite to section numbers of the brief (which are less susceptible to renumbering) rather than page numbers.

5. Multiple Revisions

If more than one person has been preparing revisions, consolidate the various versions into a single master draft for retyping. Resolve inconsistent revisions with the appropriate attorney before retyping.

B. PREPARING TABULAR MATTER

For a short legal memorandum, your work is completed when the last draft has been pronounced accurate. For lengthier memos and for petitions and briefs to be submitted to court, it will be necessary to prepare a table of contents, table of authorities, and certificate of service. If record materials are attached, it will be necessary to prepare an index to attachments. Finally, depending on court rules, it may be necessary to prepare special materials to comply with the rules of the particular court in which the document is to be filed.

1. Table of Contents

According to conventional wisdom, if any portion of a brief is to receive special attention it is the table of contents. The reason—the entire legal argument is contained in the headings, and if a judge peruses the brief no further than the table of contents, the party's message has gotten across.

There is much truth to the conventional wisdom. A skillfully written heading can be as persuasive as the carefully researched textual discussion that follows. Headings are frequently revised throughout the preparation of a brief, and it is essential that the table of contents reflects the final changes. If a table of contents is prepared at an earlier draft stage, it is important to make corresponding changes in both the text and the table. Do not make the mistake of changing one back to the former version! (To avoid such an error when there is a discrepancy, check with the author as to which version controls.)

Illustration 4 is a sample table of contents, which has been constructed by copying the headings appearing in the text and indicating the page number on which the heading appears. Note that each succeeding level of subdivision is indented and aligned. Note also that the parts of the brief are not numbered until the beginning of the argument.

ILLUSTRATION 4

TABLE OF CONTENTS

Once the table of contents has been typed, you will also want to pay attention to the following details:

(*a*) Make sure that the headings are arranged and numbered according to standard outline form. If you subdivide a section, make sure at least two subdivisions follow. Do not set forth subdivisions of a topic at the same level as that of the main topic.

(*b*) Whether the sentence or phrase format is used in the headings, make sure all headings at the same level employ the same structure (sentences or phrases). In text, be consistent in using or omitting periods after the heading.

(*c*) Make sure that whatever scheme of capitalization is employed, it is used consistently throughout the same levels. Following are suggested schemes, in descending order of subordination.

1. All letters of all words in the heading are capitalized.
2. All initial letters of all words in the heading are capitalized.
3. All initial letters of all words in the heading except articles, conjunctions, and prepositions of four letters or fewer are capitalized.
4. The sentence style of capitalization is used; that is, only the first letter of the first word and proper nouns are capitalized.

(*d*) As you revise the table of contents, make corresponding changes in the text.

EXERCISE ☐1

Use whatever stylistic changes are necessary to make the following table of contents internally consistent. Renumber the headings if necessary to express the proper level of subordination. Do not worry about page numbers.

TABLE OF CONTENTS

2. Table of Authorities

As described in Chapter 1, a table of authorities lists outside sources not developed in the record of the case under consideration. These materials are organized into types of authorities cited. The table also lists the page number on which the authorities are cited, without regard to whether the citation is in the text or a footnote.

Illustration 5 is a sample table of authorities.

ILLUSTRATION 5

TABLE OF AUTHORITIES

COURT CASES	PAGE
American Smelting & Refining Co. v. FPC, 494 F.2d 925 (D.C. Cir.), cert. denied, 419 U.S. 882 (1974)	23, 43, 56, 57
Associated Press v. United States, 326 U.S. 1 (1945), aff'g 52 F. Supp. 362 (S.D.N.Y. 1943)	23, 24, 29
California v. FPC, 369 U.S. 482 (1962)	32
Consolidated Edison Co. v. FPC, 512 F.2d 1332 (D.C. Cir. 1975)	21, 23

To compile a table of authorities, you may find it most convenient to go through the text, preparing an index card for each source cited throughout the brief. On each card, copy the citation in full, including, if applicable, prior and subsequent history, parallel citations, and citations to related authority. Do not include introductory signals or parentheticals. On cases and articles, list only the page on which the case or article begins. For books, it is not necessary to list the specific page cited.

As you compile your cards, copy down the page numbers in the brief on which the sources are cited. If a source is cited more than once throughout the brief, compare citations to make sure they are consistent. If short forms of citation are established, make sure they are adhered to once established. If a particular source is cited numerous times throughout the brief, use passim (literally, "scattered") in lieu of listing all page references.

Sources listed in the table of authorities are organized by type. There are no hard-and-fast classifications; which categories you use will depend on the quantity and types of materials cited. Following are suggested categories, together with advice for organizing the material within each category:

1. *Court cases*—List alphabetically by name of plaintiff. (NOTE: If the same case is cited variously to the lower court opinion and

to a higher court opinion, use the most complete citation, that is, cite to the lower court opinion and give subsequent history.)

2. *Agency opinions*—List alphabetically by name of plaintiff.
3. *Statutory materials*—List in order of title number. If the name of the statute is included as part of the citation, list alphabetically by name. List session laws separately in numerical order.
4. *Congressional materials (or legislative materials)*—List alphabetically.
5. *Rules and regulations* (including rules of evidence and procedure, court rules, Code of Federal Regulations, Federal Register Notices, Executive Orders)—List alphabetically by type. List C.F.R. cites and Federal Register cites in numerical order.
6. *Secondary materials (or other authorities, or miscellaneous authorities)*—List alphabetically by author; if no author, list separately by title.

If only one or two sources are cited within any of the categories, it may be advisable to group all such sources into a single miscellaneous category.

EXERCISE 2

Check the cites and Shepardize the cases in the following memorandum, and put the cites into the proper Bluebook form. Then compile a table of contents and table of authorities.

<u>MEMORANDUM OF POINTS AND AUTHORITIES</u>
<u>IN SUPPORT OF</u>
<u>MOTION TO SUPPRESS EVIDENCE</u>

I. THERE WAS NO PROBABLE CAUSE FOR THE ARREST OF THE DEFENDANT.

An arrest without a warrant by a law enforcement officer is governed in the District of Columbia by the provisions in §23 D.C. Code 581. Such an arrest will be valid when there is probable cause to believe, in the case of a misdemeanor, that a misdemeanor has been committed in the officer's presence or view. <u>Singleton</u> v. <u>United States</u>, 225 A.2d 315 (D.C.C.A. 1967). Probable cause is determined by the information available to and relied upon by the arresting officers at the time of the arrest. <u>Gatlin</u> v. <u>United States</u>, 117 U.S. App. D.C. 123, 326 F.2d 666 (1963). The test for probable cause is whether the circumstances known to a reasonably prudent police officer by personal observation amount to a misdemeanor committed or attempted in his presence or view. McDonald v. United States, 335 U.S. 451 (1948).

In the instant case, the officers were patrolling in an unmarked cruiser when they noticed the defendant riding in a taxicab in the area. The driver of the taxicab was not purported to have been driving illegally. Neither was it alleged that any of the occupants of the car, in particular the defendant, were acting in a suspicious manner. The officers' subsequent observation of an unknown male standing next to the car amounted to nothing more than a mere hunch or suspicion that criminal activity was afoot. Certainly, such information, without more, is insufficient to rise to the level of probable cause. Henry v. United States, 361 U.S. 98 (1959); Wong Sun v. United States 371 U.S. 471 (1963); Sibron v. New York 392 U.S. 40, at 934 (1968). Yet, acting on a mere hunch, the officers approached the taxicab and requested identification, and ordered the defendant out of the car. Although no formal words of arrest were spoken to Mr. Massey at the time he was ordered out of the car, the relevant inquiry as to whether an arrest occurred is what a reasonable man, innocent of any crime, would have thought had he been in the defendant's shoes. Coates v. United States, 413 F.2d 271, 134 U.S. App. D.C. 97 (D.C. Cir. 1969). It is highly relevant that the individual believed he was in the custody of the police and submitted to their power and authority. Kelley v. United States, 111 U.S. App. D.C. 296, 298 F.2d 310 (D.C. Cir. 1961).

Immediately thereafter, a search of Mr. Massey's person turned up incriminating evidence. It is settled law that the validity of a search, without probable cause to arrest, cannot be justified by what it turns up. United States v. Di Re, 332 U.S. 581 (1948).

Moreover, the facts in this case lack far fewer elements giving rise to probable cause than do the cases of Gray v. United States, 229 A.2d 153 (D.C.C.A. 1972); Waters v. United States, 311 A.2d 153 (D.C.C.A. 1973); and Sibron v. New York, supra, where the courts found no probable cause existed.

Therefore, since the arrest of Mr. Massey was illegal, the subsequent search was also unlawful, and, in turn, the weed-like substance must be suppressed as a direct fruit of unlawful police activity. Silverthorne Lumber Co. v. United States, 251 U.S. 385 (1920); Wong Sun, supra.

II. THE UNLAWFUL SEARCH CANNOT BE JUSTIFIED UNDER THE STOP AND FRISK DOCTRINE OF TERRY V. OHIO, SUPRA.

The unlawful search cannot be justified under the "stop and frisk doctrine." It is not contended that the officers were relying on a tip by a reliable source, <u>Adams</u> v. <u>Williams</u>, 407 U.S. 143 (1972); or that the defendant was under surveillance for a substantial period of time, <u>Terry</u> v. <u>Ohio</u>. Clearly, the officers were acting merely on a hunch.

Assuming, arguendo, that the officers were justified in investigating the defendant's activity, when they apprehended the car, they instructed the occupants to produce identification or submit to a search. The defendant, along with the other occupants, willingly complied with the officer's request. Once Mr. Massey produced two proper sources of identification, the police officers had no further reason to detain Mr. Massey. <u>Coleman</u> v. <u>United States</u>, 337 A.2d 767 (D.C.C.A. 1975). Next, the officers ordered the two occupants in the front seat out of the car to submit to a search. When Mr. Massey got out of the car, the officer, in blatant violation of defendant's Fourth Amendment rights against unreasonable searches, reached into Mr. Massey's coat pocket and seized a small envelope containing the weed-like substance. <u>Terry</u> would not and could not sanction the seizure and introduction into evidence of such a substance.

III. THE SEARCH CANNOT BE JUSTIFIED AS AN EXCEPTION TO THE WARRANT REQUIREMENT.

Assuming, <u>arguendo</u>, that the officers have a right to approach the car in which Mr. Massey was riding, the search and seizure does not fall within any of the carefully delineated exceptions for the requirement of a warrant. It was not a search incident to a valid arrest because it is submitted that this arrest was unlawful. See <u>Chimes</u> v. <u>California</u>, 395 U.S. 752 (1969). There was no consent to the search. See <u>Schneckloth</u> v. <u>Bustamonte</u>, 412 U.S. 219 (1973) and <u>Judd</u> v. <u>United States</u>, 278 A.2d 458. There was no hot pursuit. See <u>Warden</u> v. <u>Hayden</u>, 387 U.S. 294 (1967). Nor can the search be justified by the vehicle exception announced in <u>Pennsylvania</u> v. <u>Mimms</u>, 93 S.Ct. 330 (1978). In that case, the Court held that when an officer has lawfully detained a driver of a motor vehicle for a traffic violation, he may order the driver out of the vehicle without violating the Fourth Amendment's proscription of unreasonable searches and seizures. The <u>Mimms</u> case is distinguishable from the case at bar on two significant factors: The officer did not stop the taxicab on the basis of a traffic violation. More importantly, however, the <u>Mimms</u> case only authorizes the ordering of the driver out of the car—not the occupants. In fact, language in the opinion explicitly states that it does not tend to suggest that an officer may frisk the occupants of any car stopped for a traffic violation. Rather, that case holds only that it is permissible to order the driver out of the car. <u>Pennsylvania</u> v. <u>Mimms</u>, <u>supra</u>. Note 5 at 333. Thus, the officers lacked authority to order Mr. Massey out of the car and conduct the subsequent search.

Finally, the search cannot be justified under the plain view exception.

Such exception requires three elements: (1) the officer must be lawfully present, (2) the discovery inadvertent; and (3) the object incriminating. <u>Coolidge</u> v. <u>New Hampshire</u>, 403 U.S. 443 (1971). It is clear that the second element has not been met. The officers got out of their car and they approached the car specifically looking for drugs. Surely, they could not see within the defendant's pocket from where they were standing. It was only after they unlawfully ordered the defendant out of the car that the officers reached within the pocket and seized the substance.

CONCLUSION

Since the search does not fall within any of the exceptions, the seizure was illegal and the evidence should be suppressed.

C. OTHER DETAILS

Depending on the nature of the assignment, you may need to accomplish the following additional tasks:

1. Compile attachments or exhibits referred to in text.
2. Prepare an index to attachments or exhibits.
3. Comply with any applicable court rules.
4. Prepare and have signed a certificate of service.

The mechanics of these steps have been discussed in Chapter 1. As suggested earlier, it is a good idea to discuss these steps at the outset of the assignment so as to allow plenty of time for their preparation.

If you are working on the memo or brief itself until the deadline and cannot attend to all the last-minute details yourself, it is a good idea to prepare a checklist of remaining tasks on the day before filing, for the use of the attorney, so that nothing is overlooked at the last minute.

Once you have filed a brief in a particular forum, you may want to prepare a checklist of requirements unique to that forum for future use. You may want to include in the file a copy of the memo or brief as a sample.

9 | *Preparing the Printed Brief or Law Review Article*

This chapter describes the additional steps involved in preparing the printed brief or law review article for filing or publication. It describes the printing process and explains how to indicate the proper typeface for printed matter. It contains a chart showing the differences in typeface between typewritten and printed materials. It also illustrates the stylistic differences between a brief and a law review article. Finally, it lists emergency measures that can be taken in the event a last-minute change or correction is necessary.

If you are working on a brief or law review article that is going to be printed, there are several additional steps you will need to take.

A. DESCRIPTION OF THE PRINTING PROCESS

There are two types of printing processes that may be employed: photo offsetting of "camera-ready" copy and typesetting. With camera-ready copy, the typewritten material is photo offset and reproduced exactly as it is submitted. The quality of the final product is generally superior to the original: the printing is usually darker and clearer, and any "cut and paste" edges should not be visible in the finished product. Thus, the typed version may generally be corrected with white-out or correction tape. However, it is advisable to check with the printer prior to submission.

In materials to be typeset, a typewritten version of the brief or law review article is submitted to the printer, with additional typeface instructions marked as described later in this chapter, for setting into type. This is accomplished by essentially retyping the material into print typeface. It is not necessary for the typed manuscript to be letter perfect, as long as editorial corrections are marked neatly and clearly on the manuscript. It is advisable to submit the text double-spaced, and the footnotes (typed separately) triple-spaced.

Before sending or returning any material to a printer, always make a photocopy of the material in case of loss or destruction of the original.

In typesetting, the text and footnotes will first be reproduced separately in long strips called galleys, with the footnotes and block quotes appearing in a smaller typesize than the text.

Because the article has been completely retyped from the manuscript, when the galleys are returned for proofreading, the typewritten version must be read out loud word for word (and comma for comma) against the typeset version. Corrections are marked in the margins, using standard proofreading symbols supplied by the printer. It is important that the manuscript be read aloud, to correct any numerical errors that would not be as evident from a silent reading of the galley and to reinstate any dropped lines or misnumbered footnotes. You may also need to respond to printer's queries. The printer may request that you indicate which of the changes are due to printer's error and which are author's alterations, so that you will not be billed for printer's mistakes.

At this stage it is extremely unwise to make substantive revisions to the brief, but it is a rare author who can resist the opportunity. Be cautioned that last-minute revisions delay the printing process and create opportunity for further printing errors that will have to be corrected in an additional step. If revisions must be made, try to alter as few characters in the printed line as possible, since extensive revisions may necessitate complete resetting of subsequent lines or even the remainder of the paragraph.

The galleys will then be revised and set into numbered page proofs, with footnotes placed at the bottom of the corresponding page of the text. At this stage you should proofread the revised portions of the proofs carefully against the corrected galleys. If an entire line or lines had to be reset as a result of alterations, read the entire reset portion, making sure that no new errors were made in the resetting process. Check also to make sure that footnotes correspond to their textual references.

The page numbers of the printed brief will *not* correspond to the typewritten version. Seventy typed pages will produce approximately fifty printed pages, depending on type size, page format, margins, and the like. For this reason, you must change all internal cross references to correspond to the printed version and should not insert page numbers on the table of contents and table of authorities until the numbered page proofs are available.

Needless to say, making any but the most essential change at this point is not recommended, for the arrangement of text and footnotes may be disturbed and an additional round of proofreading will be necessary. When the page proofs are letter perfect, they will be returned to the printer for printing and binding.

B. TYPEFACE CONVENTIONS FOR PRINTED BRIEFS AND LAW REVIEW ARTICLES

The typeface to be used for printed briefs and law review articles includes regular roman type, italics, and large and small capitals. (For examples of each type, consult pages 3–5 of the Bluebook.) Boldface type may also be used for law review titles or headings or for certain features on the cover of the brief. Words that are to be italicized in print should be underlined in the typed version. Words that are to be set in large and small capitals are to be underlined with two lines for "small caps" and three lines for "large caps." If a lower-case letter is to be capitalized, underline with three lines. If an upper-case letter is to be made lower case, insert a diagonal slash through the letter.

Be aware that the typeface to be used in printed materials depends on the type of document being prepared. There is one format to follow for briefs containing in-text citations, or briefs containing in-text citations as well as footnotes. The following chart illustrates this format and highlights the differences between the typed and printed versions.

TYPE OF AUTHORITY	TYPED VERSION	PRINTED VERSION
Case names (including procedural phrases)	Underlined	Italicized
Names of reporters or loose-leaf services	Regular roman	Regular roman
Titles of hearings	Underlined	Italicized
Congressional reports	Regular roman	Regular roman
Authors of articles	Regular roman	Regular roman
Authors of books	Regular roman	Regular roman
Titles of articles	Underlined	Italicized
Titles of books	Underlined	Regular roman
Names of periodicals	Regular roman	Large and small caps
Names of newspapers	Regular roman	Regular roman
Introductory signals	Underlined	Italicized
All other authorities	Regular roman	Regular roman

When merely *referring* to an authority in text (not citing to it), titles of books, reporters, periodicals, and newspapers are italicized.

EXAMPLE: That case was reported in the now defunct <u>Federal Cases</u>.

A different format (illustrated by the following chart) is to be used for citing materials appearing in *footnotes* of law review articles. *You should be aware that a few law journals (such as <u>The Business Lawyer</u>) use ordinary roman type instead of large and small capitals or italics. Whenever possible, you should obtain a style sheet or instructions from the law review editor before embarking on a cite-checking assignment for material to be published in a law review.

TYPE OF AUTHORITY	TYPED VERSION (FOR SUBMISSION TO PRINTER)	PRINTED VERSION
Case names	Regular roman	Regular roman
Procedural phrases in case names	Underlined	Italicized

TYPE OF AUTHORITY	TYPED VERSION (FOR SUBMISSION TO PRINTER)	PRINTED VERSION
Names of reporters	Regular roman	Regular roman
Names of loose-leaf services	Regular roman (double and triple underlined)	Large and small caps
Constitutions	Regular roman (double and triple underlined)	Large and small caps
Titles of hearings	Underlined	Italicized
Congressional reports	Regular roman (double and triple underlined)	Large and small caps
Authors of articles	Regular roman	Regular roman
Authors of books	Regular roman (double and triple underlined)	Large and small caps
Titles of articles	Underlined	Italicized
Titles of books	Regular roman (double and triple underlined)	Large and small caps
Names of periodicals	Regular roman (double and triple underlined)	Large and small caps
Names of newspapers and unpublished works	Regular roman	Regular roman
Introductory signals	Underlined	Italicized

For other authorities, consult the Bluebook.

Examples of citations illustrating each format appear in the inside front cover and facing page of the Bluebook.

Finally, there are different typeface conventions for materials when they are *discussed* in a footnote (as opposed to being cited). The typeface to be used in case names appearing in footnote discussions has been set forth in detail in Chapter 3, Section B.3(c). Following is a summary of rules for textual discussions of cases and all other types of authorities:

1. Italicize case names whenever the name of only one party is given or when the full name of a case is given without any citation. At all other times, the name of the case appears in regular roman type.

2. In citing to materials other than cases, simply treat the authority as you would in *law review text* if the authority is mentioned by name only (without citation). If either a short or full citation to the authority is given, follow the typeface conventions for *law review footnotes*.

EXAMPLE: In P. Marcus, <u>Antitrust Law and Practice</u> 525 (1980), the author concludes that the government's encouragement of foreign agreements to restrict exports to the United States is "hard to reconcile with its advocacy of antitrust policies."

The format illustrated throughout the Bluebook is most helpful in preparing law review footnotes: simply adopt the typeface illustrated throughout, beginning with rule 2 on page 8. The format used throughout this book is designed to serve as a guide to preparing typewritten memoranda or briefs.

EXERCISE ☐1

Assume that the following is the text of a footnote for a law review article to be submitted to the printer. Make the appropriate markings so that the printed version will contain the proper typeface.

Though almost universally recognized, the mutuality rule received frequent criticism from both courts and commentators. As stated by Justice Traynor:

No satisfactory rationalization has been advanced for the requirement of mutuality. Just why a party who was not bound by a previous action should be precluded from asserting it as res judicata against a party who was bound by it is difficult to comprehend.

Bernhard v. Bank of Am. Trust & Sav. Ass'n, 19 Cal. 2d 807, 812, 122 P.2d 892, 895 (1942).

Nevertheless, several commentators have defended mutuality as it often may assure a just result. See 1B J. Moore, Moore's Federal Practice ¶ 0.412[1], at 1809–12 (2d ed. 1980); Moore & Currier, Mutuality and Conclusiveness of Judgments, 35 Tul. L. Rev. 301, 308–11 (1961); Seavey, Res Judicata with Reference to Persons Neither Parties nor Privies—Two California Cases, 57 Harv. L. Rev. 98, 105 (1943).

As further stated in Parklane Hosiery Co. v. Shore, 439 U.S. 322 (1979), "[d]efensive use [of collateral estoppel] occurs when a defendant seeks to prevent a plaintiff from asserting a claim the plaintiff has previously litigated and lost against another defendant." Id. at 326 n.4; accord Restatement (Second) of Judgments, § 88, comment d (Tent. Draft No. 3, 1976); Note, The Impacts of Defensive and Offensive Assertion of Collateral Estoppel by a Non-Party, 35 Geo. Wash. L. Rev. 1010 (1967).[1]

C. STYLE OF LAW REVIEW ARTICLES—TEXT AND FOOTNOTES

The main stylistic difference between briefs and law review articles is that the text of the latter is devoid of citations. Once a case or statute has been identified by name in the textual discussion, or a quotation has been given, the citation to the authority is contained in a consecutively numbered footnote. The footnotes may also contain discussions of a collateral matter, additional quotations too lengthy to include in the main discussion and exhaustive lists of background materials.

EXAMPLE: The recent case of Golden Palace, Inc. v. National Broadcasting Co.[2] held that, absent an allegation of special damages, no liability was incurred by the defendant.

> [2]386 F. Supp. 107, 109 (D.D.C. 1974), aff'd mem., 530 F.2d 1094 (D.C. Cir. 1976).

When preparing a law review article for publication, it is important that, in addition to checking the citations for accuracy and form, one should keep in mind the following points:

1. Remove all citations from the text and put them into footnotes, abbreviating case names or altering the typeface, if necessary.
2. In editing the article, the author or editor may direct textual material to be dropped to a footnote or may expand the text with material originally contained in a footnote. Be aware that such changes will affect cross references contained in other footnotes and will make it necessary to renumber the remaining footnotes.
3. Indicate the appropriate typeface to be used in printing (including in-text headings).
4. Identify block quotes as such, so that the printer will indent the quoted matter and set it in a smaller type than that used for the text.
5. Whenever a shortened form of citation is used, use the same typeface as in the full citation.
6. When proofreading the galleys, be sure to check to see that the appropriate typeface was used.
7. In composing footnotes, indent the first line of each footnote and bring succeeding lines back to the left margin (in printers' parlance, set flush with the margin). In preparing copy for the printer, set off each raised footnote number with an inverted caret.

EXAMPLE:[7]

8. In law review footnotes, you may not refer to the first authority cited in that footnote with <u>id</u>. unless the preceding footnote contained only one authority.

These fine points also pertain to a certain extent to printed briefs, although there is not the same rigidity of confining citations to the footnotes.

EXERCISE [2]

Revise the following essay so it will be suitable for publication as a printed law review article with footnotes containing citations. Move the discussion of Rhode Island and Massachusetts cases in the second paragraph from the text to a footnote following the word "constitutional" in the preceding paragraph.

During the past decade numerous courts have struck down rules prohibiting girls from playing on boys' teams in public school athletic programs. E.g., Brenden v. Independent School District, 477 F.2d 1292 (8th Cir. 1973) (high school athletic association rule prohibiting girls from engaging with boys in interscholastic athletic contests held unconstitutional); Leffel v. Wisconsin Interscholastic Athletic Association, 444 F. Supp. 1117 (E.D. Wis. 1978) (rule excluding girls from boys' teams unconstitutional unless girls' teams were established); Darrin v. Gould, 85 Wash. 2d 859, 540 P.2d 882 (1975) (exclusion of capable girls from boys' team violated equal protection regardless of existence of girls' teams). In one of the first challenges to the inevitable converse situation, the Illinois Appellate Court held in Petrie v. Illinois High School Association, 75 Ill. App. 3d 980, 394 N.E.2d 855 (1979), that preventing boys from playing on girls' volleyball teams is constitutionally permissible. Indeed, this decision indicates that a rule prohibiting male players on any girls' team would be constitutional.

Only two other states, Rhode Island and Massachusetts, have considered the constitutionality of rules prohibiting boys from playing on girls' teams. Gomes v. Rhode Island Interscholastic League, 469 F. Supp. 659 (D. R.I.), vacated as moot, 604 F.2d 733 (1st Cir. 1979); Attorney General v. Massachusetts Interscholastic Athletic Association, 1979 Mass. Adv. Sh. 1584, 393 N.E.2d 284.

Since 1975, the U.S. Supreme Court has decided a few cases involving situations where discrimination against men was claimed. See, e.g., Orr v. Orr, 440 U.S. 268 (1979) (invalidating statute allowing only women to claim alimony after a divorce); Craig v. Boren, 429 U.S. 190 (1976) (invalidating statute prohibiting sale of 3.2 beer to males under twenty-one and females under eighteen); Weinberger v. Wiesenfeld, 420 U.S. 636 (1975) (invalidating social security provision that denied payments to surviving widowers but authorized payments to widows). For a discussion of these and other sex-discrimination cases, see Ginsburg, Some Thoughts on Benign Classification in the Context of Sex, 10 Conn. L. Rev. 813 (1978); Turkington, Equal Protection of the Laws in Ilinois, 25 De Paul L. Rev. 385 (1975–1976).[2]

EXERCISE 3

As a result of heavy editing, the footnotes in this exercise need to be renumbered. In addition, revise the footnotes so that all short forms are consistent and all cross references are to the correctly numbered footnote. Where italics and large and small capitals should be used, mark the typeface appropriately.

[1] 1 W. Summers, Oil and Gas § 11, at 20 (2d ed. 1954); 10A G. Thompson, Real Property § 5319, at 684 (1957).

[2] See 1 E. Kuntz, Oil and Gas § 2.4, at 66 (1962) and 2 E. Kuntz, Oil and Gas § 18.2 (1964).

[4] R. Hemingway, Oil and Gas § 6.1 (1971); 10A Thompson, supra note 1, § 10.26, at 580; 1 H. Williams & C. Meyers, Oil and Gas Law § 209, at 96 (Supp. 1969); see, e.g., Connell v. Kanwa Oil, 161 Kan. 649, 170 P.2d 631 (1946). But see 2 Kuntz, supra note 2, § 18.2, at 4, where it is observed that, "[i]n states which follow the common law, difficulty is encountered in any attempt to identify the property rights and relationship between the parties created by the oil and gas lease with any single established concept.

[5] 4 E. Kuntz, Oil and Gas § 50.1, at 261 (1972); 1 H. Williams & C. Meyers, supra note 4, § 218; G. Thompson, supra note 1, § 5329, at 742.

[6] L. Jones, Easements § 1, at 3 (1898); 2 G. Thompson, Real Property, § 315, at 2 (1961); 2 E. Washburn, Real Property, § 1225, at 273 (6th ed. 1902).

[7] Jones, supra note 6, § 49, at 38; 1 E. Washburn, Easements and Servitudes 3 (4th ed. 1885); 1 G. Thompson, Real Property § 139, at 523 (1964); 3 H. Tiffany, Real Property § 839, at 427 (3d ed. 1939) [hereinafter cited as 3 Tiffany].

[9] 2A Thompson, supra note 6, § 316, at 16, 22.

[10] See 1 Thompson, supra note 7, § 139, at 524; 2 G. Thompson, supra note 6, at § 315; 3 Tiffany, supra note 7, § 840, at 429.

[11] 3 Tiffany, Real Property, supra note 7, § 840, at 429.

[12] See 1 Thompson, supra note 7, § 139, at 524; 2 Thompson, supra note 6, § 316, at 22; 3 Tiffany, supra note 3, § 840, at 429.

[13] Jones, supra note 6, at 4; 2 Washburn, supra note 6, Real Property, § 1227; 2 Thompson, supra note 6, § 315, at 7, 8.

[14] Washburn, supra note 7, § 1, at 2; 2 Thompson, supra note 6, § 316, at 16.

[15] L. Jones, Easements, infra note 6, § 49, at 38; Washburn, Easements, supra note 7, § 1, at 3; 1 Thompson, supra note 7, § 139, at 523.[3]

D. PREPARING THE COVER

A final detail that must be taken care of in filing a printed brief is preparing a cover and choosing the color. As noted in Chapter 1, some courts designate the use of a particular color to signify the status of the party filing the brief. Experienced printers are generally aware of these requirements. If no particular color is mandated, the parties should coordinate color selection in advance, to avoid duplication, particularly if several parties filing separate briefs are involved, such as codefendants, intervenors or amicus curiae. You should also be aware of margin and paper size requirements, as well as page limitations, the number of copies required for service and filing, and filing deadline.

The law firm or printer can probably provide you with a sample brief, from which you can prepare the typewritten cover page. Then, working from the printed sample, mark the cover to show the desired typeface. Boldface type is designated "Bf." The cover should be as carefully proofread as the text.

E. IF AN ERROR OCCURS

No matter how carefully you prepare your project, through haste, inadvertence, or fatigue, errors may appear in the final product, or a significant opinion may be handed down during the final press run. For errors or new developments resulting in serious inaccuracies, you may consider the following remedial measures:

1. Having the printer prepare an errata sheet to be affixed to the front of the brief or article.
2. Preparing a boxed notice to be placed at the end of the article or brief, where there may be blank space available. This will avoid the necessity of deleting or renumbering footnotes to accommodate the new information.
3. Preparing stickers to be placed by hand over the erroneous matter.
4. Rerunning the sheets containing the pages to be corrected.
5. Filing the brief within the deadline and filing an amended brief as soon as possible thereafter.

Above all, try not to panic. Both printers and clerks of the court are used to last-minute problems and are prepared to deal with them. Your goal is to file or publish an accurate finished product.

Notes

CHAPTER 2

1. Reprinted from *Shepard's Atlantic Reporter Citations*, August 1981 Annual Cumulative Supplement, p. 528, with permission of the copyright holder. Copyright 1981 by McGraw-Hill, Inc.
2. The references in the following section to materials appearing in *U.S. Law Week*, vol. 48, pp. 3046, 3214, 3219, were made with permission of the copyright holder. Copyright 1979 by the Bureau of National Affairs.

CHAPTER 3

1. Reprinted with revisions from the *Florida State University Law Review*, vol. 8, p. 54, n. 49, with permission of the copyright holder. Copyright 1980 by the *Florida State University Law Review*.

CHAPTER 7

1. Reprinted with revisions from the *Houston Law Review*, vol. 17, p. 847, n. 61, with permission of the copyright holder. Copyright 1980 by the *Houston Law Review*.
2. Ibid., p. 826, n. 290.
3. Ibid., pp. 801–2, n. 159.
4. Ibid., pp. 802–3, n. 166.
5. Ibid., p. 802, n. 166.
6. Ibid., p. 806, n. 183.
7. Ibid., p. 807, n. 183.
8. Ibid., p. 807, n. 185.
9. Ibid., p. 825, n. 281.
10. Ibid., p. 826, n. 291.
11. Ibid., p. 826, n. 297.
12. Ibid., p. 876, n. 18.
13. Reprinted with revisions from the *Marquette Law Review*, vol. 64, p. 141, n. 36, with permission of the copyright holder. Copyright 1980 by the *Marquette Law Review*.
14. Reprinted with revisions from the *Harvard Law Review*, vol. 95, p. 1481, n. 113, with permission of the copyright holder. Copyright 1982 by the *Harvard Law Review*.
15. Ibid., p. 1916, n. 11.
16. Ibid., p. 1480, n. 107.
17. Ibid., p. 1952, n. 100.
18. Reprinted with revisions from the *Georgia Law Review*, vol. 15, p. 393, n. 72, with permission of the copyright holder. Copyright 1981 by the *Georgia Law Review*.
19. *Houston Law Review*, vol. 17, p. 837, n. 9.
20. Ibid., p. 868, n. 179.
21. *Harvard Law Review*, vol. 95, p. 1917, n. 15.
22. *Houston Law Review*, vol. 17, p. 795, n. 115.
23. Adapted from the *Marquette Law Review*, vol. 64, p. 230, nn. 37, 38, with permission of the copyright holder. Copyright 1980 by the *Marquette Law Review*.
24. Reprinted with revisions from the *Harvard Law Review*, vol. 95, p. 778, n. 101, with permission of the copyright holder. Copyright 1982 by the *Harvard Law Review*.

25. Reprinted with revisions from the *Loyola University of Chicago Law Journal*, vol. 12, p. 238, n. 36, with permission of the copyright holder. Copyright 1981 by the *Loyola University of Chicago Law Journal*.
26. Ibid., p. 211, n. 10.
27. Ibid., p. 279, n. 7.
28. Ibid., p. 155, n. 147.
29. Ibid., p. 141, n. 54.
30. *Georgia Law Review*, vol. 15, p. 378, n. 10.
31. *Loyola University of Chicago Law Journal*, vol. 12, p. 141, n. 55.
32. Ibid., p. 216, n. 31.
33. Ibid., p. 278, n. 5.
34. Ibid., p. 143, n. 67.
35. Ibid., p. 262, n. 51.
36. *Georgia Law Review*, vol. 15, p. 470, n. 9.

CHAPTER 9

1. Reprinted with revisions from the *John Marshall Law Review*, vol. 14, p. 203, nn. 7, 11, with permission of the copyright holder. Copyright 1980 by the *John Marshall Law Review*.
2. Ibid., p. 227.
3. Reprinted with revisions from the *Oklahoma Law Review*, vol. 33, pp. 430–32, nn. 1–15, with permission of the copyright holder. Copyright 1980 by the *Oklahoma Law Review*.

GLOSSARY

Throughout this book, or in the course of working on cite-checking assignments, you may encounter numerous terms that are not defined in the text or whose meanings are not readily apparent from the context. In order to make the learning task smoother, these terms have been assembled and defined for your convenience.

Advance sheets A preliminary paperback version of a publication that is prepared in advance of the permanent edition.

Appendix In briefs or memoranda, a compilation of record materials cited therein and included as part of the submission to the court.

Bill A legislative proposal, introduced by one or both houses of Congress, which may lead to the enactment of a statute.

Block quotation A direct quotation of fifty words or more, which is indented and set off from the rest of the text. In printed materials, the block quotation is set in a smaller typeface than the surrounding text.

Bluebook Popular name for *A Uniform System of Citation*, published by the Harvard Law Review Association, containing the rules of citation for legal authorities.

Blurb Brief summary of a case holding, usually contained in a parenthetical following the case citation.

Case at bar The case in support of which a brief or memorandum is being submitted. Synonymous with "instant case," "case at hand."

Citation The setting forth, either in a footnote or in the text of a legal writing, of the source of authority for a statement made or quotation given. Synonymous with "cite" (used as a noun).

Cite To present a legal authority as support for a statement, argument, or quotation.

Codification Compilation of laws currently in force, organized by numbered titles or subject-matter codes arranged alphabetically.

Committee print Legislative study published by a congressional committee.

Ellipsis The deliberate omission of a word or words in a direct quotation, indicated by the insertion of three periods (separated by spaces).

Emphasis The use of underlining or italics to call attention to a significant passage; may appear in the original text or be added by the one quoting the material.

Galleys Long strips of printed matter prepared by the printer as a first step in the printing process.

Headnotes Consecutively numbered entries appearing at the beginning of a reported case, prepared by the publisher, consisting of summaries of the case's holding on a particular point of law.

Hereinafter A word used to introduce a special shortened form of a citation to a particular work, beginning with the next citation to that authority.

Id. Latin abbreviation for a word meaning "in the same place," which may in most situations be used as a short form for citing to the immediately preceding authority.

Infra Latin for "below"; used to refer to a full citation appearing later on in the work.

Introductory signal A word or phrase used to introduce citations that indicates the type and degree of support the cited authorities give to the preceding statement.

Jump cite The second page number given in a full citation to a legal authority; this page contains the statement or quotation for which the material is cited (also called "pinpoint cite").

Loose-leaf service Publication appearing in loose-leaf form, which contains useful information on a specialized topic, such as regulations, opinions, agency releases, case summaries, and the like.

Mem. Abbreviation for "Memorandum"; a term used to indicate the disposition of a case (e.g., affirmed, reversed, and so on) without an opinion; not to be confused with "memorandum opinion," a term some judges use to refer to their written opinions.

Official source Opinions or statutes published by a court, government agency, or the like.

Opinion below In an appellate proceeding, reference to the opinion of a lower court from which an appeal is being taken.

Ordinance Enactment of a city, county, or other local entity.

Page proofs Unbound printed material arranged in the form in which it will appear in print.

Pagination System of numbering pages consecutively within a given work, subdivision of a work, or successive issues of a work.

Paperbound supplement A separately printed paperback volume of a publication that is designed to update material appearing in an earlier published, permanently bound volume.

Parallel citation A citation to a second source that also contains the cited matter.

Parenthetical An explanation of, or a quotation from, the cited source that is appended to the main citation.

Per curiam A term used to designate an opinion of an appellate court for which no member of the court claims authorship (literally, "for the court").

Petition for certiorari Application to an appellate court for permission to present the case on appeal. "Certiorari" is abbreviated "cert."

Pinpoint cite See definition of "jump cite."

Pocket part A separately printed update to a publication, which is inserted into the inside back cover of the bound volume to which it relates.

Preferred unofficial source Source indicated by the Bluebook as the source to be cited if the official source is unavailable.

Proposition Assertion made in a legal memorandum or brief, supported by one or more legal authorities.

Record Pleadings, transcripts, and so on filed with the court or agency in the course of a given proceeding.

Regulation A rule promulgated by a federal, state, or local agency and having the force of law.

Reporter A publication that reprints opinions of agencies or courts of a given jurisdiction or level.

Resolution A proposal introduced by one or both houses of Congress, which may be adopted as introduced.

Restatement A publication based on case law in a specified area of the law, defining the evolving consensus of the law in that area.

Session laws Compilation of laws in chronological order of enactment.

Shepardizing Systematic use of *Shepard's Citations* to ascertain the history of a case or to locate subsequent citations to that case.

Sic Latin for "so" or "thus"; a term inserted into a quoted passage when an error appears in the original, to indicate that the original source is being reproduced exactly as it appears.

Slip opinion Opinion published by the issuing court or agency (to be cited if no published version is available).

Statute Legislative enactment of a state legislature or the U.S. Congress.

Stet Latin for "let it stand." In proofreading, this symbol is used to instruct the typist or printer that the handwritten revision is to be ignored and the original material printed.

String citation Lengthy or exhaustive list of authorities used to support a statement made in the text of a brief, memorandum, law review article, or treatise.

Supra Latin for "above"; used to refer to a full citation appearing earlier in the work.

Syllabus A brief summary of the holding of a case appearing at the beginning of the official version of the case, which has been prepared by the clerk of the court.

Table of authorities List of all legal authorities cited in a brief or memorandum.

Transfer binder A semi-permanent binder to which pages of a loose-leaf service are kept prior to being permanently bound.

Treatise Single-volume or multivolume scholarly work on a broad area of the law.

Uniform acts Legislation on a particular matter drafted by the National Conference of Commissioners on Uniform State Laws, which is adopted by various states and included in the state code.

Unofficial source Publication of a case or statute by a commercial publisher, generally available sooner than official sources.

Unreported case Case not appearing in any published source, in which instance the slip opinion issued by the court or agency would be cited.

Index to Exercises

Answer Key

CHAPTER 1

EXERCISE ⬚1⬚

NOTE: Since the memorandum did not indicate the date of the transcripts, it is also correct to place the November and December transcripts prior to the March transcripts.

STATEMENT OF FACTS

On October 10, 1977, Appellant was initially arrested by officers of the Metropolitan Police Department. (March 21 Tr. 140, App. at 5) Appellant was originally arrested at his home on a charge of assault. (Mar. 21 Tr. 188, App. at 6) This charge arose out of an incident that took place on the evening of October 7, 1977, and early morning of October 8, 1977 (Mar. 21 Tr. 5, App. at 3), and involved Ms. Edna McConnell, the complainant, who had known Appellant for several years prior to the evening of that night. (Mar. 21 Tr. 6, App. at 4)

Beginning on October 11, 1977, Appellant was represented by John Drury, Esq. However, Mr. Drury's appearance was for the limited purpose of presentment only (Dec. 6 Tr. 3, App. at 18), and the trial court appointed Grandison Hill, Esq., on October 21, 1977, to represent the Appellant. On November 29, 1977, Mr. Drury formally withdraw his appearance by praecipe and notified the trial court in person at the Appellant's arraignment on December 6, 1977, in CR 88377-77. (Dec. 6 Tr. 4, App. at 19).

While the case jacket indicates that Appellant was scheduled for arraignment in CR 88377-77 on November 29, 1977, the hearing held at that time was termed a "status hearing." (Nov. 29 Tr. 2, App. at 17) There was no plea entered in the matter until December 6, 1977. (Dec. 6 Tr. 5, App. at 20) By the time of the November 29, 1977 "status hearing" Appellant had already been in contact with Mr. Hill, his newly appointed counsel. In arguing for a mental examination, counsel noted that he had "several conversations" with Appellant. (Nov 29 Tr. 2, App. at 17) Despite this preliminary contact, or perhaps because of it, the Appellant became apprehensive about counsel's effectiveness in his case. As a consequence, Appellant filed a pro se motion alleging, inter alia, ineffectiveness of counsel. (See Appendix A, Petition for Hearing, R. 23)

At the arraignment hearing in CR 88377-77, held on December 6, 1977, appointed counsel was again not present to represent Appellant due to a friend's unspecified medical problems. (Dec. 6 Tr. 3, App. at 18) It should be noted that counsel also failed to appear for at least one hearing prior to the December 6th arraignment. (Nov. 29 Tr. 2, App. at 17) By a fortunate circumstance, Appellant's prior counsel, Mr. Drury, was present in court to explain the earlier appointment of Mr. Hill. (Dec. 6 Tr. 3, App. at 18) Thus, Mr. Drury stood in for appointed counsel at Appellant's arraignment on December 6, 1977. (Dec 6 Tr. 4, App. at 19)

Although Appellant's trial was set for February 17, 1978 (Dec 13 Tr. 4, App. at 21), because of the inability to complete the tests as required by the trial court, Appellant's trial was not begun until March 20, 1978. (See letters at R. 136–138)

At trial, the government presented several witnesses. The major witness was Ms. Edna McConnell, the complainant, who recounted the events of October 7th and 8th of 1977. (Mar. 20 Tr. 5, App. at 1) She testified concerning the threats which she said Appellant had made to her that evening. (Mar. 20 Tr. 18, App. at 2) The government presented testimony from several acquaintances of Appellant, as well as the police officers who initially arrested Appellant. The government also presented physical evidence and photographs to support its case.

The Appellant testified in his own behalf and presented two additional witnesses. During the Appellant's testimony, he denied he threatened the complainant (Mar. 21 Tr. 233, App. at 7), and stated that at the time of the event he was in an alcoholic stupor. (Mar. 21 Tr. 249, App. at 8) The defense also presented the testimony of Appellant's wife (Mar. 22 Tr. 337, App. at 11) and Doctor Leonard Maitland of the District's Forensic Psychiatry Division. (Mar. 22 Tr. 313, App. at 9)

Dr. Maitland submitted a report which found Appellant competent to stand trial and indicated that his actions were not the product of mental illness. (See Appendix B, Defendant's Exhibit 2, R. 151) This report was received, without government objection, by the trial court as part of Appellant's case in chief. (Mar. 22 Tr. 316, App. at 10) Dr. Maitland also indicated in his report that Appellant's behavioral controls "were probably impaired at the time of the offense" by alcohol. (Appendix B, paragraph 5)

After two and one half days of deliberation, the jury found Appellant not guilty of obstructing justice (Mar. 28 Tr. 391, App. at 13) and reported a deadlock on the assault charge. (Mar. 28 Tr. 390, App. at 12) The jury did find the Appellant guilty of the charge of threats. (Mar. 28 Tr. 391, App. at 13) Appellant's counsel then requested a jury poll on the guilty verdict of threats. The first juror questioned on the "threats" verdict announced "not guilty." (Mar. 28 Tr. 391, App.

at 13) The trial court proposed to continue the poll over the Appellant's objection. (Mar. 28 Tr. 391, App. at 13) After it was explained what a jury poll is designed to do, the first juror then announced "guilty." (Mar. 28 Tr. 392, App. at 14) The court concluded that the verdict was unanimous. (Mar. 28 Tr. 394, App. at 15) It also declared a mistrial as to the deadlocked assault charge. (Mar. 28 Tr. 394, App. at 15)

Appellant was scheduled to be sentenced on May 12, 1978. (Mar. 28 Tr. 395, App. at 16) On May 9, 1978, Mr. Hill was allowed to withdraw as counsel by the trial court, "at the defendant's request." (R. 7, 8) New Counsel was appointed and Appellant was sentenced on May 11, 1978, to 4–12 years on the charge of threats. Appellant filed a pro se notice of appeal on May 18, 1978.

> NOTE: It would also be proper to adapt the id. form throughout this exercise, whenever the citations are taken from the same transcript. For example, if the first citation in a paragraph is to "Mar. 28 Tr. 391, App. at 13," and the following citation is to "Mar. 28 Tr. 390, App. at 12," the following form may be substituted: "Id. 390, App. at 12."

EXERCISE 2

1. United States Court of Appeals for the District of Columbia Circuit
2. continuance
3. five
4. attorney
5. civil
6. 13
7. the party's telephone number
8. bar number

EXERCISE 3

INDEX TO APPENDIX

PAGE

Opinion, p. 3
Record, pp. 1, 15–19, 45, 47, 60, 61, 68, 70, 73–77, 140, 152–54, 159, 177, 178, 196, 206, 209, 210, 227, 229, 250, 261, 266, 267, 270
Plaintiff's Exhibits 1, 2, 6

STATEMENT OF FACTS

Appellants in this action are Amy Young and Thomas Young t/a The American Food Store, hereinafter referred to as the "Thomases" or "American Food Store" or Defendants. Appellees in this action are 1800 Connecticut Avenue Joint Venture, hereinafter "1800 Connecticut Avenue Joint Venture" or "Plaintiff" where appropriate. The Record will be referred to as "R" followed by the corresponding page number in the transcript. The Court's Opinion will be referred to as "O" followed by the corresponding page number.

In July 1978, 1800 Connecticut Avenue Joint Venture purchased two adjacent parcels of real property in the District of Columbia, 1800 Connecticut Avenue and 2031 Florida Avenue, from Dr. Melvin McCarthy, his wife and his mother, May McCarthy. [R-15, 60, 61, 73]

Prior to July 1978, 1800 Connecticut Avenue was owned by Dr. Melvin McCarthy and his wife. [R-60, 61] Prior to July 1978, the real property located at 2031 Florida Avenue was subject to a life interest in Mrs. May McCarthy with the remainder interest in her son, Dr. Melvin McCarthy. [R-73]

The Thomases began renting the property at 1800 Connecticut Avenue from Dr. Melvin McCarthy beginning May 1, 1974, at a rent of $225 a month. [R-16, 18, 45, 75; Plaintiff's Exhibit 1] The lease contained an option to renew for another three-year term at a monthly rental which was to be determined at the expiration of the lease. [Plaintiff's Exhibit 1] In June 1977, the rent was increased to $250/month. [R-261] The lease of the American Food Store was for three years and expired on April 30, 1977. [R-1, 16, 18; Plaintiff's Exhibit 1]

After April 30, 1977, the Thomases became month-to-month tenants. [R-17, O-3] The Thomases did not exercise their option to renew their lease for another three-year term. [R-16, 47, 74, 267]

The property adjacent to the American Food Store, 2031 Florida Avenue, was rented by William Nathan and Perry White from May 4, 1974, to April 30, 1975, and operated under the name of American Bazaar. [R-1, 159; Plaintiff's Exhibit 6] When Nathan and White left, the Thomases continued paying rent. [R-206]

On November 30, 1978, 1800 Connecticut Avenue Joint Venture gave the Thomases a 30-day notice to vacate. [R-18, 19; Plaintiff's Exhibit 2] At the time of the trial, May 16, 1979, the Thomases were still in possession of the subject property. [O-3]

On April 8, 1978, the Thomases went to the residence of Mrs. McCarthy and asked her for a lease covering the premises at both 1800 Connecticut Avenue and 2031 Florida Avenue. [R-68, 177, 178] It was undisputed that Defendants owed back rent on both of the properties. [R-76, 77, 209, 210]

One Hundred Ten Dollars was due her son, Dr. Melvin McCarthy, for the eleven months that the American Food Store was paying $240/month rent instead of $250/month for the property located at 1800 Connecticut. [R-70, 74] Eighteen Hundred Ten Dollars was due on the property at 2031 Florida Avenue for back rent to which Mrs. May McCarthy was entitled. [R-140, 209, 166]

According to the Thomases' testimony and that of William Nathan, Mrs. McCarthy promised them a lease if they would pay the back rent. [R-153, 196, 270] The Thomases gave Mrs. May McCarthy a check for $110 for the back rent on 1800 Connecticut Avenue which was deposited to the account by her son. [R-229] The Thomases sent Mrs. McCarthy a check for $1,810 for back rent on 2031 Florida Avenue for the American Bazaar. [R-250]

Mrs. May McCarthy never gave them the lease. [R-152, 153] Furthermore, no rent of $500 a month was ever paid for the leasing of the two properties subsequent to the April 1978 meeting. [R-154, 227]

On November 30, 1978, 1800 Connecticut Avenue Joint Venture Associates gave the Thomases the 30-day notice to vacate. [R-18, 19] This appeal followed.

EXERCISE 4

1. Federal Rules of Appellate Procedure
2. marked by asterisks
3. all parties and amici who appeared in the proceeding below
4. an appendix or addendum to the brief
5. appellants
6. U.S. App. D.C. Reports
7. 50
8. 7

CHAPTER 2

EXERCISE ☐1

1. 288 P. 555 (Kan. 1930). (Note: The Pacific Digest table of cases does not cover cases in the first series. The answer to this problem was located by consulting the case index to Volume 288 of the Pacific Reporter.)
2. 436 F. Supp. 743. (Note: The fact that a district court was cited in the parenthetical should alert you to the fact that the citation to the reporter was inaccurate.)
3. 494 F.2d 270 (3d Cir.), cert. denied, 419 U.S. 883 (1974). (Note: As indicated in the table of cases to the Modern Federal Practice Digest, the name of the case was changed on appeal to United States v. Bankers Trust Co. The name change was not indicated in the citation because it was on a denial of certiorari. You would, however, need to know this information in order to locate it in U.S. Reports [for verification purposes].)
4. 223 F. Supp. 215 (E.D. Okla. 1963).
5. 625 F.2d 1206 (5th Cir. 1980), cert. denied, 449 U.S. 1089 (1981).

EXERCISE ☐2

1. 430 U.S. 144 (1977).
2. 408 U.S. 665 (1972).
3. 446 U.S. 14 (1980).
4. 87 Wis. 2d 819, 275 N.W.2d 723 (1979).
5. 71 App. Div. 2d 1014, 420 N.Y.S.2d 414 (1979).
6. 22 Cal. 3d 552, 586 P.2d 162, 150 Cal. Rptr. 129 (1978).
7. 612 F.2d 292 (7th Cir. 1979). (If you consulted Modern Federal Practice Digest, you would be confused, because the court citation was improper. The index to 1980–1 Trade Cases (CCH) contained the correct citation.)
8. 314 N.E.2d 549 (Ill. App. Ct. 1974).
9. 399 F. Supp. 1062 (N.D. Ill. 1975), aff'd, 539 F.2d 712 (7th Cir. 1976).
10. 447 F. Supp. 221 (D.D.C. 1979), remanded, 604 F.2d 698 (D.C. Cir. 1979).

EXERCISE ③

1. 261
2. (*a*) run into text
   (*b*) indented and single-spaced
3. (*a*) no ¶
   (*b*) ¶
4. (*a*) [I]t is entirely proper...
   (*b*) "It is not consonant with the amenities...of the administration"
   (*c*) [¶] "Both statutory provisions under which petitioner was prosecuted permit conviction upon proof of the defendant's possession of narcotics ...."
   (*d*) To establish "standing," Courts of Appeals have generally required that the movant claim either to have owned or possessed the seized property or to have had a substantial possessory interest in the premises searched.... [A]"
   (*e*) Change all single quotation marks to double quotation marks.
   (*f*) On direct examination he testified that the apartment belonged to a friend, Evans, who had given him the use of it, and a key, with which petitioner had admitted himself on the day of the arrest....
   ....
   In affirming petitioner's conviction the Court of Appeals agreed with the District Court that petitioner lacked standing,
5. "Exective" becomes "[effective]."
6. "Both statutory provisions under which petitioner was prosecuted [26 U.S.C. § 4704(a) and 21 U.S.C. § 174] permit conviction upon proof of the defendant's possession of narcotics ...."
7. "The sole evidence upon which the warrant was issued was an affidavit signed by [Officer] Didone."
8. "Rule 41(e) should not be applied to allow the Government to deprive the defendant of standing to bring a motion to suppress by framing the indictment in general terms, while prosecuting for possession." Jones v. United States, 362 U.S. 257, 264–65 (1960) (footnote deleted).
9. Jones v. United States, 362 U.S. 265 n.1 (1960).
10. "The restrictions upon searches and seizures, [are] obviously designed for protection against official invasion of privacy and the security of property."

11. Rakas v. Illinois, 439 U.S. 128, 169 (1978) (White, J., dissenting) (emphasis in original).

12. Jones v. United States, 362 U.S. 257, 261 (1960) (emphasis added).

13. [A] motion to suppress, under Rule 41 (e), must be made prior to trial, if the defendant then has knowledge of the grounds on which to base the motion. The government argues that the defendant therefore must establish his standing to suppress the evidence at that time through affirmative allegations and may not wait to rest standing upon the Government's case at the trial. This provision of Rule 41(e) ... is a crystalization of decisions of this Court requiring that procedure, and is designed to eliminate from the trial disputes over police conduct not immediately relevant to the question of guilt. Jones v. United States, 362 U.S. 257, 264 (1960) (citations omitted).

EXERCISE 4

1. In re Penn Central Securities Litigation, 416 F. Supp. 907 (E.D. Pa. 1976), rev'd, 560 F.2d 1138 (3d Cir. 1977).

2. United States v. Hinds County School Board, 560 F.2d 1188 (5th Cir. 1977), cert. denied, 435 U.S. 951 (1978). (Note that the name changed on appeal. The Supreme Court citation was verified by reference to the circuit court opinion.)

3. In re Namenson, 555 F.2d 1067 (1st Cir.), cert. denied, 434 U.S. 866 (1977).

4. Tamari v. Bache Halsey Stuart, Inc., 619 F.2d 1196 (7th Cir.), cert. denied, 449 U.S. 873 (1980).

5. Intercounty Construction Corp. v. Walter, 422 U.S. 1 (1975).

6. Alexander v. HUD, 441 U.S. 39 (1979).

7. Lauritzen v. Chesapeake Bay Bridge & Tunnel District, 259 F. Supp. 633 (E.D. Va. 1966), aff'd in part and rev'd in part, 404 F.2d 1001 (4th Cir. 1968). (Note: Shepard's indicated that the lower court opinion was modified on appeal. The opinion itself contained further clarifying language.)

8. Daniel v. Waters, 399 F. Supp. 510 (M.D. Tenn. 1975), vacated and remanded, 515 F.2d 485 (6th Cir. 1975). (Note: Shepard's merely indicated that the 6th Circuit opinion was the "same case" as the one reported in 399 F. Supp. 510.)

9. In re Penn Central Securities Litigation, 347 F. Supp. 1327 (E.D. Pa. 1972), aff'd, 494 F.2d 528 (3d Cir. 1974).

10. Whitney v. California, 274 U.S. 357 (1927), overruled, 395 U.S. 444 (1969). (Note that Shepard's gave only the pinpoint cite. The first page of the case must be obtained by examining the case itself. The author should be queried as to whether a case that has been overruled should be cited at all, unless it is mentioned for historical purposes.)

EXERCISE 5

1. Penix v. Richardson, 468 F.2d 1259 (9th Cir. 1972), cert. denied, 410 U.S. 986 (1973).

2. Goodbody & Co. v. Penjaska, 8 Mich. App. 64, 153 N.W.2d 665 (1967), cert. denied, 393 U.S. 16 (1968).

3. Platzman v. American Totalisator Co., 45 N.Y.2d 910, 383 N.E.2d 876, 411 N.Y.S.2d 230 (1978), aff'g 57 App. Div. 2d 753, 57 App. Div. 2d 755, 394 N.Y.S.2d 412, 560 (1977).

4. No change.

5. Marshall v. District of Columbia, 392 F. Supp. 1012 (D.D.C. 1975), aff'd, 559 F.2d 726 (D.C. Cir. 1977).

6. No change.

7. United States v. Napoli, 530 F.2d 1198 (5th Cir.), cert. denied, 429 U.S. 920 (1976).

EXERCISE 6

1. Stegall v. United States, 153 F. Supp. at 850.

2. Eisen I; Eisen II; Eisen II, 479 F.2d at 1110.

3. Deaton v. Vise, 186 Tenn. at 365, 210 S.W.2d at 666.

4. Id. § 1640(a)(2).

5. Doe v. Poelker, 515 F.2d at 548.

6. Id. at 548.

7. Id. § 322.

8. 192 Tenn. at 407, 241 S.W.2d at 510.

9. Id. at 439.

10. Human Rights Hearings at 388.

CHAPTER 3

EXERCISE $\boxed{1}$

1. No change.
2. Indiana State Employees Association v. Boehning.
3. United States v. 11 Acres of Land.
4. Commissioner v. Weinrich's Estate.
5. In re Committee of Censors of the Philadelphia Bar Association.
6. Kentucky ex rel. Kern v. Maryland Casualty Co.
7. Commonwealth ex rel. Toliver v. Ashe.
8. Connecticut Fire Insurance Co. v. Reliance Insurance Co.
9. No change.
10. Town of Bristol v. United States ex rel. Small Business Administration.

EXERCISE $\boxed{2}$

1. Tom W. Carpenter Equip. Co. v. GE Credit Corp.
2. Indiana State Employees Ass'n v. Boehning.
3. United States v. 11 Acres of Land.
4. Commissioner v. Weinrich's Estate.
5. In re Committee of Censors of the Philadelphia Bar Ass'n. (Note: It would also be correct to abbreviate "Philadelphia" as "Phila.")
6. Kentucky ex rel. Kern v. Maryland Cas. Co.
7. Commonwealth ex rel. Toliver v. Ashe.
8. Connecticut Fire Ins. Co. v. Reliance Ins. Co.
9. No change.
10. Town of Bristol v. United States ex rel. SBA.

EXERCISE $\boxed{3}$

1. Cross Key, 372 So. 2d at 918. Although a Florida appellate court in Albrecht v. Department of Envt'l Regulation, 353 So. 2d 883, 887 (Fla. Dist. Ct. App. 1978), has stated that the 1974 Florida Administrative Procedure Act provides an "array of procedural safeguards

[and] has lessened the need for strict statutory standards in the delegation of power to administrative agencies," that position has not been followed by the Florida Supreme Court. At one time, it seemed that then Justice (now Chief Justice) England of the Florida Supreme Court was about to adopt the modern position:

> In summary, I conceive that the Legislature has lawfully delegated to the executive branch the enforcement of its announced policy in this area. There is no abuse of that delegation so long as the class of prohibited acts are more specifically defined by prospective administrative action to which the Administrative Procedure Act applies.

Department of Legal Affairs v. Rogers, 329 So. 2d 257, 269 (Fla. 1976) (England, J., concurring). However, Chief Justice England's concurring opinion in Cross Key is diametrically opposed to the Davis view:

> Justice Sundberg [the author of the Askew v. Cross Key Water-ways opinion] has revitalized a vastly more important doctrine—one that guarantees that Florida's government will continue to operate only by consent of the governed. He is saying, quite simply, that whatever may be the government predilections elsewhere, in Florida no person in one branch of our government may by accident or by assignment act in a role assigned by the Constitution to persons in another branch.

372 So. 2d at 925. Then, however, in Department of Business Regulation v. National Manufactured Hous. Fed'n, 370 So. 2d 1132, 1137 (Fla. 1979), the Chief Justice concurred in the result only. Although all this may lead one to speculate about the Chief Justice's position, the recent cases indicate that the position of the Florida Supreme Court cannot be questioned. See, e.g., Florida Home Builders Ass'n v. Division of Labor, 367 So. 2d 219 (Fla. 1979).

EXERCISE 4

1. FPC v. Amerada Petroleum Corp.
2. Axton Candy & Tobacco Co.

3. Environmental Defense Fund, Inc. v. HEW.
4. Myers v. Commissioner.
5. Atlanta & St. Andrews Bay Ry. Co.

EXERCISE 5

1. Eastern Air Lines v. United States, 132 F. Supp. 787.
2. Early v. Heath, 170 F.2d 70 (4th Cir.), aff'g 77 F. Supp. 474.
3. Garlinger v. Garlinger, 137 N.J. Super., 347 A.2d 801.
4. In re Marriage of Lusk, 86 Cal. App. 3d 228, 150 Cal. Rptr. 63.
5. Frank Lyon Co. v. United States, 435 U.S. 561, 584 (Stevens, J., dissenting). (Note: Page 584 is retained as the pinpoint cite.)

EXERCISE 6

1. Go Getter Tug, 398 F.2d 873.
2. Eastern Motor Export v. United States, 344 U.S. 298. (Note: This was tricky. The opinion was captioned "American Trucking Associations v. United States." A footnote to the opinion reveals that the principal case was heard along with Eastern Motor Export and another case. The Index to Cases in U.S. Reports includes Eastern Motor Export as an entry.)
3. Greenberg v. Union National Bank, 5 N.D. 483, 67 N.W. 597.
4. People v. Miller, 39 A.D.2d 893, 334 N.Y.S.2d 252.
5. State v. Crudup, 176 N.J. Super. 215, 422 A.2d 790.

EXERCISE 7

1. Lewis v. Pennington, 257 F. Supp. 815 (E.D. Tenn.), aff'd in part and rev'd in part, 400 F.2d 806 (6th Cir.), cert. denied, 393 U.S. 983.
2. Parker v. Anderson-Prichard Oil Corp., 245 F.2d 831 (10th Cir.).
3. Crown Aluminum Industries Corp. v. NLRB, 352 F.2d 84 (3d Cir.).
4. In re Crown Cartridge Corp., 220 F. Supp. 914 (S.D.N.Y.).
5. Eli Lilly & Co. v. Brenner, 375 F.2d 599 (D.C. Cir.).

EXERCISE 8

1. G & S Land, Transp. & Development Corp. v. Yarbrough, 153 Ga. App. 644, 266 S.E.2d 508 (Ct. App.).
2. Bouvia v. Atlantic Testing Laboratory, 50 A.D.2d 680, 375 N.Y.S.2d 204 (App. Div.).
3. People v. Dalton, 24 Cal. 3d 850, 598 P.2d 467, 157 Cal. Rptr. 497.
4. Morton v. United States, 415 A.2d 800 (D.C.).
5. Alexander & Alexander, Inc, v. Central Penn Nat'l Bank, 421 A.2d 220 (Pa. Super. Ct.).

EXERCISE 9

1. Blake v. City of Los Angeles, 595 F.2d 1367 (9th Cir. 1979), cert. denied, 100 S. Ct. 1865 (1980).
2. Fullilove v. Beame, 48 N.Y.2d 376, 398 N.E.2d 765, 423 N.Y.S.2d 144 (Ct. App. 1979).
3. Stevens v. Airline Pilots Ass'n Int'l, 413 A.2d 1305 (D.C. 1980), cert. denied, 49 U.S.L.W. 3511 (U.S. Jan. 20, 1981).
4. United States v. Mar-Tee Contractors, Inc., 6 Envtl. L. Rep. (Envtl. L. Inst.) 20,417 (D.N.J. Jan. 28, 1976).
5. State v. Matsen, 26 Crim. L. Rep. (BNA) 2313 (Ore. Oct. 23, 1979).

CHAPTER 4

EXERCISE 1

1. S. 3323, 83d Cong., 2d Sess. (1954).
2. H.R.J. Res. 555, 83d Cong., 2d Sess. (1954).
3. H.R. Rep. No. 2639, 83d Cong., 2d Sess. (1954).
4. S. 3323 and H.R. 8862 to Amend the Atomic Energy Act of 1946: Hearings Before the Joint Comm. on Atomic Energy, 83d Cong., 2d Sess. 25 (1954) (statement of Jerome D. Luntz).
5. 100 Cong. Rec. 4933 (1954).

EXERCISE ☐2

1. Arlington County, Va., Zoning Ordinance § 19 (1980).
2. Exec. Order No. 12,235, 45 Fed. Reg. 58,803 (1980).
3. 45 Fed. Reg. 58,837 (1980) (to be codified at 21 C.F.R. pt. 182).
4. Treas. Reg. § 346.2.
5. Exec. Order No. 11,805, 39 Fed. Reg. 34,261 (1974), reprinted in 26 U.S.C. § 6103 note (1976).
6. Interview with the President, 16 Weekly Comp. Pres. Doc. 239 (Jan. 29, 1980).
7. Fed. R. App. P. 45(a).
8. 8 C.F.R. § 245.4 (1980).
9. Va. Sup. Ct. R. 3A:21.

CHAPTER 5

EXERCISE ☐1

1. U.S. Const. amend. XXI, § 2.
2. Food Stamp Act Amendments of 1980, § 111, Pub. L. No. 96-249, 94 Stat. 357, 7 U.S.C.A. § 2012 (West 1980).
3. Pub. L. No. 96-265, 94 Stat. 453 (June 9, 1980) (effective June 1, 1981).
4. 26 U.S.C. § 7851 (1976 & Supp. III 1979).
5. Rail Passenger Service Act of 1970, 45 U.S.C. § 562 (1976), as amended by Passenger Railroad Rebuilding Act of 1980 (amending scattered sections of 45 U.S.C.), 45 U.S.C.A. § 562 (West Supp. 1980).
6. Restatement (Second) of Agency, § 407, at 255 (1958).

EXERCISE ☐2

1. Tex. Rev. Civ. Stat. art. 16.25 (Vernon 1963 & 1980 Supp.).
2. Pub. Act No. 81-1456, 1980 Ill. Legis. Serv. (West).
3. Alabama Worthless Check Act, Ala. Code § 13-4-110 (1977).
4. Cal. Bus. & Prof. Code § 16,200 (Deering 1976).
5. Me. Rev. Stat. Ann. tit. 9B, § 313 (West Supp. 1978).

EXERCISE ③

1. R 94 St 2240, A 88 St 1 440. Repealed at 94 Statutes at Large 2240, amended at 88 Statutes at Large 440.
2. L 87 St 99. Provisions of an existing statute declared not to be extended in its application to a later statute. This would not affect the basic citation.
3. C 531 F 2d 491, C 439 FS 261. Upheld as constitutional in two cited cases. This would not affect the basic citation.
4. A & Rn Subsec [b 94 St 2921. Amended and renumbered as sub-section (b) at 94 Statutes at Large 2921.
5. Ad 87 St 221. The cited provision was added by an enactment appearing at 87 Statutes at Large 221. This would not affect the citation.

CHAPTER 6

EXERCISE ①

1. Nat'l Comm'n on the Causes and Prevention of Violence, Firearms and Violence in American Life 111 (1969).
2. C. White III, Writing Effective Proposals 17–20 (ABA Special Comm. on Youth Education for Citizenship. The $$ Game, Working Notes No. 7, 1975).
3. Million, Racial Restrictive Covenants Revisited, in Open Occu-pancy vs. Forced Housing Under the Fourteenth Amendment 95 (A. Avins ed. 1963).
4. The Criminal Law A-81 (D. Nedrud & M. Oberto ed. 1971).
5. H. Edwards & V. Nordin, Higher Education and the Law 16 (Cum. Supp. 1980).
6. 9 J. Wigmore, Wigmore on Evidence, § 2461, at 187 (3d ed. 1940).
7. Burns, Foreword to White Justice (S. Blackburn comp. 1971). (Note: This book consists of a series of trial transcripts; hence a compiler rather than an author is named.)

EXERCISE 2

1. Newspaper
2. Periodical
3. Loose-leaf
4. Newspaper
5. Newspaper

6. Periodical
7. Loose-leaf
8. Periodical
9. Periodical
10. Newspaper

EXERCISE 3

1. Creighton L. Rev.
2. U. West L.A. L. Rev.
3. Inst. on Sec. Reg.
4. B.C. Indus. & Com. L. Rev.
5. Fordham Urb. L.J.
6. Geo. Wash. J. Int'l L. & Econ.
7. Trial Law. Q.
8. Ottawa L. Rev.
9. Colum. J. Transnat'l L.
10. Notre Dame Law

EXERCISE 4

1. Note, Constitutional Law—First Amendment—Advertising of Prescription Drug Prices as Protected Commercial Speech, 18 B.C. Indus. & Com. L. Rev. 276 (1977).
2. Gamer, Agent's Privilege to Interfere Intentionally with Contractual Relations: A Reappraisal of California Law, 12 Cal. W.L. Rev. 475 (1976).
3. Civil and Political Rights of Aliens in the U.S.S.R.: A Survey of Soviet Legislation, 11 Tex. Int'l L.J. 571 (1976).
4. Wilbur, Book Review, 20 Am. J. Legal Hist. 155 (1976) (reviewing L. Baker, John Marshall: A Life in Law (1974).
5. Nuclear Power Symposium, 6 Envtl. Law 322 (1976).
6. Bibliography, 9 J. Crim. L., Criminology & Police Sci. 235 (1955).

7. Annot., 3 A.L.R.2d 682 (1949).
8. Rose, Checkless Banking Is Bound to Come, Fortune, June 1977, at 118.
9. Petersen & Stillman, Phencyclidine Abuse, 5 Drug Enforcement 19 (1978).
10. Special Section—Regulated Industries in Virginia and the 1977 General Assembly, 18 Wm. & Mary L. Rev. 73 (1976).

EXERCISE ⑤

1. Rose, Trudeau's Plan to Rewrite Constitution Goes to Canada's Supreme Court Today, Wall St. J., Apr. 28, 1981, at 15, col. 1.
2. Lewis, West Africa's Creeping Democracy, N.Y. Times, May 4, 1981, at A23, col. 5.
3. Tufaro Transit Co. v. Board of Education of New York, N.Y.L.J., Mar. 26, 1981, at 1, col. 6 (S.D.N.Y. Mar. 11, 1981).
4. Democratic Chief Seeks Probe of Right-Wing PACs, Christian Science Monitor, May 6, 1981, at 2, col. 2.
5. L.A. Times, Sept. 23, 1979, pt. III, at 4, col. 1.

EXERCISE ⑥

1. Tumey v. Crown Central Petroleum Corp., Antitrust & Trade Reg. Rep. (BNA) No. 963 (May 8, 1980), at E-1.
2. Transcontinental Gas Pipe Line Corp., FPC Dkt. No. CP78-463, F.E.R.C. Rep. (CCH) ¶ 62,193 (Nov. 21, 1980).
3. Pacific Intermountain Express Co. v. ICC, 1979 Fed. Carr. Cas. (CCH) ¶ 82,819 (9th Cir.).
4. United States Parole Comm'n v. Gerahty, 26 Crim. L. Rep. (BNA) 3139 (Mar. 19, 1980).
5. [1980–1981 Transfer Binder] Stauffer Chem. Co. v. FDA, Food Drug Cosm. L. Rep. (CCH) ¶ 38,065, at 38,303 (C.D. Cal. 1980).
6. SEC v. Brigadoon Scotch Distrib. Co., [1973 Transfer Binder] Fed. Sec. L. Rep. (CCH) ¶ 94,017 (S.D.N.Y. 1973).

EXERCISE ⑦

1. M. Gottlieb, The Anti-Nazi Boycott Movement in the American Jewish Community 1933–1941 (April 1967) (unpublished Ph.D. dissertation for Brandeis University, University Microfilm No. 67-16,553).

2. Address by Robert Stipe, Conference on Preservation Law, Washington, D.C., May 1, 1971, at 6–7 (unpublished speech).

3. Appellant's Brief at 25, Coalition for Lower Beaufort County v. Alexander, No. 77–1866 (D.C. Cir. filed Jan. 26, 1978).

4. Interview with Stephany Madsen, Managing Editor, Land Development Law Reporter, at the Land Development Institute, Washington, D.C. (Apr. 20, 1982).

5. Remarks of Labor Solicitor Carin Clauss, Conference on Equal Employment and Collective Bargaining, excerpted in Washington Memorandum, Corporate Practice Series (BNA) No. 84, at 1 (May 27, 1980).

CHAPTER 7

EXERCISE ①

1. Watts v. United States, 394 U.S. 705 (1969) (remark made during political debate expressly conditioned on event not expected to occur not a threat against President in violation of 18 U.S.C. § 871(a)).

2. See also Thornhill v. Alabama, 310 U.S. 88, 102–03 (1940) (purely informational union picketing entitled to constitutional protection). Note: No change is necessary. The parenthetical and pinpoint cite are both accurate.)

3. See United States v. South-Eastern Underwriters Ass'n, 322 U.S. 533, 553–60 (1944) (insurance industry fell within ambit of the Sherman Act, even though the Court had ruled prior to 1890 that insurance was not commerce and therefore was subject to court

regulation). (Note: The text of page 565 (dissenting opinion) reaches the opposite conclusion.)

4. The Court subsequently elaborated on its definition of boycott in terms of commercial objectives in St. Paul Fire & Marine Insurance Co. v. Barry, 438 U.S. 531, 543–44 (1978). In that case, the Sherman Act was held to apply where the plaintiff had induced its competitors to refuse to deal on any terms with its customers in order to keep its policyholders from obtaining alternative sources of coverage, and even from negotiating for more favorable terms elsewhere. Although the boycotters and their targets were not involved in competitive relationships with each other, the Court held that the Sherman Act was still violated because of the horizontal agreement among the parties to stop selling to particular customers. (Note: This "blurb" is too lengthy for a parenthetical. The spare language of the parenthetical was expanded, and connective terms were added for clarity.)

5. Another case in which the Court has recognized that expressive conduct is protected under the first amendment is Eisenstadt v. Baird, 405 U.S. 438, 460 (1972) (Douglas, J., concurring). (Note: Do not give the page on which the concurring opinion begins.)

EXERCISE 2

1. For an extensive discussion of the difficulties inherent in regulating carcinogens and the consequent necessity of making policy choices, see McGarity, Substantive and Procedural Discretion in Administrative Resolution of Science Policy Questions: Regulating Carcinogens in EPA and OSHA, 67 Geo. L.J. 729 (1979).

2. The term "under color of law" was initially interpreted to mean that the plaintiff must demonstrate that his constitutional rights were violated pursuant to the enforcement of a statute or ordinance. E.g., Lane v. Wilson, 307 U.S. 268 (1939) (damages awarded to blacks who were denied the right to vote by a discriminatory state

statute); Hague v. CIO, 307 U.S. 496 (1939) (city ordinance prohibited public meetings and distribution of printed materials).

3. In general, where other actions have not been commenced, class action treatment is deemed proper. See, e.g., Fidelis Corp. v. Litton Industries, 293 F. Supp. 164, 171 (S.D.N.Y. 1968). (Note: Fidelis is precisely on point. Hohmann does not state that the lack of other actions was a factor in its decision.)

4. The Clean Water Act allows an aggrieved state to bring a direct action against the administrator for failure to enforce federal or state discharge requirements in a neighboring state. See, e.g., Illinois v. City of Milwaukee, 406 U.S. 91, 101–08 (1972).

5. There is a split among the circuits as to whether the federal common-law nuisance doctrine is applicable to actions brought under the Clean Water Act. Compare Evansville v. Kentucky Liquid Recycling Corp., 604 F.2d 1008, 1016 (7th Cir. 1979) (private rights of action prohibited under the Act) with National Sea Clammers Ass'n v. City of New York, 616 F.2d 1222 (3d Cir. 1980), where the Third Circuit upheld an implied private right of action under the Clean Water Act.

EXERCISE ③

1. 4	2. 8	3. 7	4. 5	5. 6
6. 3	7. 1	8. 10	9. 2	10. 9

EXERCISE ④

1. (a) 9	2. (a) 2	3. (a) 15
(b) 6	(b) 5	(b) 14
(c) 7	(c) 4	(c) 10
(d) 8	(d) 3	(d) 11
	(e) 1	(e) 13
		(f) 12

CHAPTER 8

EXERCISE ☐1

TABLE OF CONTENTS

EXERCISE 2

MEMORANDUM OF POINTS AND AUTHORITIES IN SUPPORT OF MOTION TO SUPPRESS EVIDENCE

I. THERE WAS NO PROBABLE CAUSE FOR THE ARREST OF THE DEFENDANT.

An arrest without a warrant by a law enforcement officer is governed in the District of Columbia by the provisions in D.C. Code Ann. § 23-581 (1981). Such an arrest will be valid when there is probable cause to believe, in the case of a misdemeanor, that a misdemeanor has been committed in the officer's presence or view. Singleton v. United States, 225 A.2d 315 (D.C. 1967). Probable cause is determined by the information available to and relied upon by the arresting officers at the time of the arrest. Gatlin v. United States, 326 F.2d 666 (D.C. Cir. 1963). The test for probable cause is whether the circumstances known to a reasonably prudent police officer by personal observation amount to a misdemeanor committed or attempted in his presence or view. McDonald v. United States, 335 U.S. 451 (1948).

In the instant case, the officers were patrolling in an unmarked cruiser when they noticed the defendant riding in a taxicab in the area. The driver of the taxicab was not purported to have been driving illegally. Neither was it alleged that any of the occupants of the car, in particular the defendant, were acting in a suspicious manner. The officers' subsequent observation of an unknown male standing next to the car amounted to nothing more than a mere hunch or suspicion that criminal activity was afoot. Certainly, such information, without more, is insufficient to rise to the level of probable cause. Sibron v. New York, 392 U.S. 40 (1968); Wong Sun v. United States, 371 U.S. 471 (1963); Henry v. United States, 361 U.S. 98 (1959). Yet, acting on a mere hunch, the officers approached the taxicab and requested identification, and ordered the defendant out of the car. Although no formal words of arrest were spoken to Mr. Massey at the time he was ordered out of the car, the relevant inquiry as to whether an arrest occurred is what a reasonable man, innocent of any crime, would have thought had he been in the defendant's shoes. Coates v. United States, 413 F.2d 371 (D.C. Cir. 1969). It is highly relevant that the individual believed he was in the custody of the police and submitted to their power and authority. Kelley v. United States, 298 F.2d 310 (D.C. Cir. 1961).

Immediately thereafter, a search of Mr. Massey's person turned up incriminating evidence. It is settled law that the validity of a search, without probable cause to arrest, cannot be justified by what it turns up. United States v. Di Re, 332 U.S. 581 (1948).

Moreover, the facts in this case lack far fewer elements giving rise to probable cause than do the cases of Gray v. United States, 292 A.2d 153 (D.C. 1972); Waters v. United States, 311 A.2d 835 (D.C. 1973); and Sibron v. New York, 392 U.S. 40 (1968), where the courts found no probable cause existed.

Therefore, since the arrest to Mr. Massey was illegal, the subsequent search was also unlawful, and, in turn, the weedlike substance must be suppressed as a direct fruit of unlawful police activity. Wong Sun v. United States, 371 U.S. 471 (1963); Silverthorne Lumber Co. v. United States, 251 U.S. 385 (1920).

II. THE UNLAWFUL SEARCH CANNOT BE JUSTIFIED UNDER THE STOP AND FRISK DOCTRINE OF TERRY v. OHIO.

The unlawful search cannot be justified under the "stop and frisk doctrine." It is not contended that the officers were relying on a tip by a reliable source, Adams v. Williams, 407 U.S. 143 (1972); or that the defendant was under surveillance for a substantial period of time, Terry v. Ohio, 392 U.S. 1 (1968). Clearly, the officers were acting merely on a hunch.

Assuming, arguendo, that the officers were justified in investigating the defendant's activity, when they apprehended the car, they instructed the occupants to produce identification or submit to a search. The defendant, along with the other occupants, willingly complied with the officer's request. Once Mr. Massey produced two proper sources of identification, the police officers had no further reason to detain Mr. Massey. Coleman v. United States, 337 A.2d 767 (D.C. 1975). Next, the officers ordered the two occupants in the front seat out of the car to submit to a search. When Mr. Massey got out of the car, the officer, in blatant violation of defendant's Fourth Amendment rights against unreasonable searches, reached into Mr. Massey's coat pocket and seized a small envelope containing the weedlike substance. Terry would not and could not sanction the seizure and introduction into evidence of such a substance.

III. THE SEARCH CANNOT BE JUSTIFIED AS AN EXCEPTION TO THE WARRANT REQUIREMENT.

Assuming, arguendo, that the officers have a right to approach the car in which Mr. Massey was riding, the search and seizure does not fall within any of the carefully delineated exceptions for the requirement of a warrant. It was not a search incident to a valid arrest because it is submitted that this arrest was unlawful. See Chimel v. California, 395 U.S. 752 (1969). There was no consent to the search. See Schneckloth v. Bustamonte, 412 U.S. 218 (1973) and Robinson v. United States, 278 A.2d 458 (D.C. 1971). There was no hot pursuit. See Warden v. Hayden, 387 U.S. 294 (1967). Nor can the search be justified by the vehicle exception announced in Pennsylvania v. Mimms, 434 U.S. 106 (1977). In that case, the Court held that when an officer has lawfully detained a driver of a motor vehicle for a traffic violation, he may order the driver out of the vehicle without violating the Fourth Amendment's proscription of unreasonable searches and seizures. The Mimms case is distinguishable from the case at bar on two not insignificant factors: The officer did not stop the taxicab on the basis of a traffic violation. More importantly, however, the Mimms case only authorizes the ordering of the driver out of the car—not the occupants. In fact, language in the opinion explicitly states that it does not tend to suggest that an officer may frisk the occupants of any car stopped for a traffic violation. Rather, that case holds only that it is permissible to order the driver out of the car. Pennsylvania v. Mimms, 434 U.S. at 110 n.5. Thus, the officers lacked authority to order Mr. Massey out of the car and conduct the subsequent search.

Finally, the search cannot be justified under the plain view exception. Such exception requires three elements: (1) the officer must be lawfully present, (2) the discovery inadvertent; and (3) the object incriminating. Coolidge v. New Hampshire, 403 U.S. 443 (1971). It is clear that the second element has not been met. The officers got out of their car and they approached the car specifically looking for drugs. Surely, they could not see within the defendant's pocket from where they were standing. It was only after they unlawfully ordered the defendant out of the car that the officers reached within the pocket and seized the substance.

CONCLUSION

Since the search does not fall within any of the exceptions, the seizure was illegal and the evidence should be suppressed.

TABLE OF CONTENTS

TABLE OF AUTHORITIES

Chapter 9

EXERCISE ①

Though almost universally recognized, the mutuality rule received frequent criticism from both courts and commentators. As stated by Justice Traynor:

No satisfactory rationalization has been advanced for the requirement of mutuality. Just why a party who was not bound by a previous action should be precluded from asserting it as res judicata against a party who was bound by it is difficult to comprehend.

Bernhard v. Bank of Am. Trust & Sav. Ass'n, 19 Cal. 2d 807, 812, 122 P.2d 892, 895 (1942).

Nevertheless, several commentators have defended mutuality as it often may assure a just result. See 1B J. Moore, Moore's Federal Practice ¶ 0.412[1], at 1809–12 (2d ed. 1980); Moore & Currier, Mutuality and Conclusiveness of Judgments, 35 Tul. L. Rev. 301, 308–11 (1961); Seavey, Res Judicata with Reference to Persons Neither Parties Nor Privies—Two California Cases, 57 Harv. L. Rev. 98, 105 (1943).

As further stated in Parklane Hosiery Co. v. Shore, 439 U.S. 322 (1979), "[d]efensive use [of collateral estoppel] occurs when a defendant seeks to prevent a plaintiff from asserting a claim the plaintiff has previously litigated and lost against another defendant." Id. at 326 n.4; accord Restatement (Second) of Judgments, § 88, Comment d (Tent. Draft No. 3, 1976); Note, The Impacts of Defensive and Offensive Assertion of Collateral Estoppel by a Non-Party, 35 Geo. Wash. L. Rev. 1010 (1967).

EXERCISE 2

During the past decade numerous courts have struck down rules prohibiting girls from playing on boys' teams in public school athletic programs.[1] In one of the first challenges to the inevitable converse situation, the Illinois Appellate Court held in Petrie v. Illinois High School Association[2] that preventing boys from playing on girls' volleyball teams is constitutionally permissible. Indeed, this decision indicates that a rule prohibiting male players on any girls' team would be constitutional.[3]

Since 1975, the U.S. Supreme Court has decided a few cases involving situations where discrimination against men was claimed.[4]

---

[1]E.g., Brenden v. Independent School District, 477 F.2d 1292 (8th Cir. 1973) (high school athletic association rule prohibiting girls from engaging with boys in interscholastic athletic contests held unconstitutional); Leffel v. Wisconsin Interschol. Athletic Ass'n, 444 F. Supp. 1117 (E.D. Wis. 1978) (rule excluding girls from boys' teams unconstitutional unless girls' teams were established); Darrin v. Gould, 85 Wash. 2d 859, 540 P.2d 882 (1975) (exclusion of capable girls from boys' team violated equal protection regardless of existence of girls' teams).

[2]75 Ill. App. 3d 980, 394 N.E.2d 855 (1979).

[3]Only two other states, Rhode Island and Massachusetts, have considered the constitutionality of rules prohibiting boys from playing on girls' teams. Gomes v. Rhode Island Interschol. League, 469 F. Supp. 659 (D.R.I.), vacated as moot, 604 F.2d 733 (1st Cir. 1979); Attorney General v. Massachusetts Interschol. Athletic Ass'n, 79 Mass. Adv. Sh. 1584, 393 N.E.2d 284 (1979).

[4]See, e.g., Orr v. Orr, 440 U.S. 268 (1979) (invalidating statute allowing only women to claim alimony after a divorce); Craig v. Boren, 429 U.S. 190 (1976) (invalidating statute prohibiting sale of 3.2 beer to males under twenty-two and females under eighteen); Weinberger v. Wiesenfeld, 420 U.S. 636 (1975) (invalidating social security provision that denied payments to surviving widowers but authorized payments to widows). For a discussion of these and other sex-discrimination cases, see Ginsburg, Some Thoughts on Benign Classification in the Context of Sex, 10 Conn. L. Rev. 813 (1978); Turkington, Equal Protection of the Laws in Illinois, 25 De Paul L. Rev. 385 (1975–1976).

EXERCISE ⬚3

[1]1 W. Summers, Oil and Gas § 11, at 20 (2d ed. 1954); 10A G. Thompson, Real Property § 5319, at 684 (1957).

[2]See 1 E. Kuntz, Oil and Gas § 2.4, at 66 (1962) and 2 E. Kuntz, Oil and Gas § 18.2 (1964).

[3]R. Hemingway, Oil and Gas § 6.1 (1971); 10A Thompson, supra note 1, § 10.26, at 580; 1 H. Williams & C. Meyers, Oil and Gas Law § 209, at 96 (Supp. 1969). See, e.g., Connell v. Kanwa Oil, 161 Kan. 649, 170 P.2d 631 (1946). But see 2 Kuntz, supra note 2, § 18.2, at 4, where it is observed that, "[i]n states which follow the common law, difficulty is encountered in any attempt to identify the property rights and relationship between the parties created by the oil and gas lease with any single established concept."

[4] 4 E. Kuntz, Oil and Gas § 50.1, at 261 (1972); 1 Williams & Meyers, supra note 3, § 218; G. Thompson, supra note 1, § 5329, at 742.

[5] L. Jones, Easements, § 1, at 3 (1898); 2 G. Thompson, Real Property, § 315, at 2 (1961); 2 E. Washburn, Real Property, § 1225, at 273 (6th ed. 1902).

[6] Jones, supra note 5, § 49, at 38; 1 E. Washburn, Easements and Servitudes 3 (4th ed. 1885); 1 G. Thompson, Real Property § 139, at 523 (1964); 3 H. Tiffany, Real Property, § 839, at 427 (3d ed. 1939).

[7] 2 Thompson, supra note 5, § 316, at 16, 22.

[8] See 1 Thompson, supra note 6, § 139, at 524, and 2 Thompson, supra note 5, § 315; 3 Tiffany, supra note 6, § 840, at 429.

[9] 3 Tiffany, supra note 6, § 840, at 429.

[10] See 1 Thompson, supra note 6, § 139, at 524, and 2 Thompson, supra note 5, § 316, at 22; 3 Tiffany, supra note 6, § 840, at 429.

[11] Jones, supra note 5, at 4; 2 Washburn, supra note 5, § 1227; 2 Thompson, supra note 5, § 315, at 7, 8.

[12] Washburn, Easements, supra note 6, § 1, at 2; Jones, supra note 5, § 1, at 3; 2 Thompson, supra note 5, § 316, at 16.

[13] Jones, supra note 5, § 49, at 38; Washburn, Easements, supra note 6, § 1, at 3; 1 Thompson, supra note 6, § 139, at 523.

Index

blurbs (explanatory
    parentheticals), 133-34, 140,
    143
Board of Tax Appeals, 66
book reviews, citations of, 114
books, citations of, 103-10
brackets
    for omissions at beginning of
      quotations, 26
    to show textual alternations in
      quotations, 28-30
briefs
    citations of, 129
    covers for, 177
    errors in, 177-78
    final details for, 165
    parts of, 2-3
    preparing tabular matter for,
      155-62
    printing, 167-69
    putting text into final form for,
      153-44
    record materials in, 3-5
    typeface conventions for, 169-72
business names, 59-60
but cf., 142-43
but see, 142

California, citations for cases
    from, 19
capitalization style, 158
cases
    cited from newspapers, 123
    citing, 53
    citing prior and subsequent
      history of, 41-44
    courts and jurisdictions for,
      70-74
    dates for, 74-76
    reporters on, information on,
      67-69
    Shepardizing, 34-40
    short forms for citations of,
      45-46
    typeface conventions for, 172
    see also names of cases

cf., 140, 141
    but cf., 142-43
circuit courts, federal, 70
citations, 13
    of administrative cases and
      arbitrations, 66-67
    of books and pamphlets, 103-10
    of briefs, motions and
      memoranda, 129
    of case names in law review
      footnotes, 61-64
    of case names in text, 54-60
    of cases, 53
    of constitutions, 87-88
    correct, finding, 14-16
    courts and jurisdictions in,
      70-74
    dates in, 74-76
    direct quotations in, 22-30
    of federal statutes, 88-95
    as footnotes in law review
      articles, 173-74
    information on reporters in,
      67-69
    of legislative history materials,
      77-82
    of loose-leaf services, 124-28
    of newspapers, 121-23
    official, finding, 17-22
    order within, 136, 145-50
    parentheticals in, 131-34
    of periodicals, 111-21
    of prior and subsequent case
      histories, 41-44
    of quasi-statutory materials,
      82-86
    Shepardizing cases and, 34-40
    short forms for, 45-51
    of state statutes, 98
    of statutes, *Shepard's* for, 100-2
    structure of, 145
    to support text statements,
      136-44
    of unpublished materials, 129-30
city names, 58-59
Code of Federal Regulations, 83

secondary authorities, 135
secondary sources, for federal
    statutes, 90-91
Securities and Exchange
    Commission (SEC), 19
see, 139
    but see, 142
see also, 140
see generally, 143
Senate (U.S.)
    bills in, 77-78
    committee prints by, 81
    debates in, 81
    hearings in, 79
    reports by, 80
    resolutions in, 78-79
series numbers, for books cited,
    106-7
session laws, 90
Shepardizing cases, 34-38
    U.S. Law Week for, 38-40
Shepard's Acts by Proper Names, 101
Shepard's Atlantic Reporter
    Citations, 34-37
    for different case names, 43
Shepard's Citations to Statutes,
    100-1
short forms for citations
    for cases, 45-46
    to reduce inconsistencies, 154
    for statutes, 46-47
    use of "hereinafter" in, 50-51
    use of *id.* in, 47-48
    use of *supra* and *infra* in, 48-50
"sic," 28
signals
    citations without, 137
    introductory, 137-44
    order of, 145-46
    order of authorities within,
    147-50
simple resolutions (legislative), 78
slip laws, 88
spacing
    in names of periodicals, 117-18
    in names of reporters, 68

specially reproduced materials, 21
speeches, presidential, 85
star editions, of books cited, 107
state courts
    citations of cases before, 71-72
    forms for state names in cases
    before, 58
    official citations of opinions
    of, 19
    official and unofficial reporters
    for, 17
states
    constitutions of, 87-88
    statutes of, 96-98
statements of facts (in briefs), 3
    record materials in, 3-5
statutes
    federal, 88-95
    legislative history materials
    for, 77-82
    quasi-statutory materials, 82-86
    Shepard's citations to, 100-2
    short forms for citations of,
    46-47
    state, 96-98
Statutes at Large, 85, 89, 91
structure of citations, 145
style
    of capitalization, 158
    for quotations, 24-25
    of text and footnotes for law
    review articles, 173-74
sub nom. form, 44
subsequent histories of cases,
    42-43
supplements, to treatises, 109
supra, 48-50
    used with "hereinafter," 51
Supreme Court, U.S.
    editors of older reporters for,
    68
    memorandum decisions by, 41
    naming, in citations, 71
    rules for official citations for,
    17-18
    Shepardizing cases to, 37

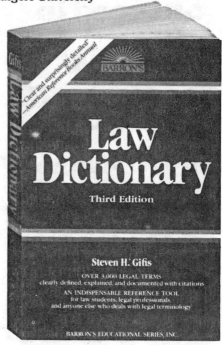